AUTOMATING THE NORTHERN LINE

AUTOMATING THE NORTHERN LINE

OWEN SMITHERS

AMBERLEY

First published 2016

Amberley Publishing
The Hill, Stroud
Gloucestershire, GL5 4EP

www.amberley-books.com

British Library Cataloguing in Publication Data.
A catalogue record for this book is available from the British Library.

ISBN 978 1 4456 5482 9 (print)
ISBN 978 1 4456 5483 6 (ebook)

Typeset in 10pt on 13pt Sabon.
Typesetting and Origination by Amberley Publishing.
Printed in the UK.

Contents

Chapter One

In the Beginning

A group of farsighted investors got together and formed the City of London & Southwark Subway company on 28 July 1884. Their aim was to build a small bore tunnel, with a 10-foot diameter, through which electric locomotives, drawing special coaches, would transport passengers from South London into the city. The City & South London railway was the first deep-level underground 'tube' railway in the world, and the first major railway in the world to use electric traction. Originally it was intended for cable-hauled trains, but the financial collapse of the cable contractor while the railway was under construction forced a change to electric traction before the line opened – an experimental technology at the time. Under the direction of pioneer engineer, James Henry Gatehead, digging was started to provide twin tunnels from Stockwell to Monument (King William Street) – a total of 3.25 miles.

Fourteen electric locomotives were ordered from Mather & Platt Ltd in Manchester and delivered during 1889. Later locomotives were supplied by Compton Ltd. Meanwhile, under an Act of Parliament, the company's name was changed to the City & South London Railway company (C&SLR), still retaining its own financial control.

On 25 July 1890, they took delivery of thirty coaches and test-running commenced. Each train was made up of three coaches. The coaches seated thirty-two passengers on two facing seats, upholstered, and the coaches had no windows, since it was felt that, there being nothing to see they were not required to see, hence the nickname of 'padded cells'. Each car contained sliding doors or gates at each end, which were attended by a gateman. Sixteen candlepower lamps lighted each coach and one car was retained for smoking only, a car from which ladies were forbidden. A notice

This is the C&SLR electric locomotive, built by Mather & Platt Ltd, who supplied the first fourteen in 1889.

Locomotive No. 10 was named *Princess of Wales* in readiness for the royal opening ceremony. It had a special plate affixed to this effect. The opening was performed by Edward VII, then Prince of Wales, on 4 November 1890, with the line being opened to the public on 18 December 1890.

An electric locomotive with a single coach, known as the 'padded cell', since it had no windows. Exit at stations was via the single end.

in each car stated that riding on the roof was forbidden, the penalty being a forty-shilling fine. There seems to be no record of anyone trying it.

The line proved so popular that thought was given to extending the line northwards into the city itself. Work was commenced, tunnelling towards Moorgate, which was opened in February 1900. This involved closing the original terminus at King William Street, sealing off the tunnels under the Thames. This involved swinging the new tunnels over each other to reach the Bank station, as the trait at the time was to build the tunnels above each other. The northbound tunnels eventually became the left tunnel to Moorgate. Tunnelling had also been going on south of Stockwell and the line was eventually opened to Clapham Common in June 1900.

To put into effect the traffic operation on this line meant a locomotive always pulled. In order to carry on with this practise, the first train had a locomotive at each end. When reaching the end of line, the first locomotive was uncoupled and, when its original train departed, it was shunted in readiness to couple to the next arriving train and so forth through out the day.

A Mr Harry Newstead joined the C&SLR in 1902 as a box boy at Stockwell. He worked ten hours a day for ¼d a day. He explained that all the trains at both ends of the line were stabled in the tunnels; it was also where they were cleaned. He was later promoted to cleaner at 2s 6d a day. His progression through the grades was first as signalman, then guard and, finally, motorman. He was transferred to Morden in 1926 when the extension had been completed, where he remained until his retirement in 1954. He was offered the chance to stay on in a lower grade and he accepted a stationman's position. In the mid-1960s, he was my box boy many times at Morden signal box when I covered duties there. It was he who supplied me with a view of what it was like working on the C&SLR in the 1900s, which I found invaluable.

Meanwhile, another railway group was formed in August 1893 with the title of the Charing Cross, Euston & Hampstead Railway Company. Their intention was to build a tube railway from the centre of London out to the countryside of North London. Work was started from the Strand, then called Charing Cross, which had the first reversing loop on the line; it emerged out to the single northbound platform at the present-day Embankment and proceeded north to Hampstead and Archway, which was

LER trailer car RG 207. These were built by a number of companies, notably the American Car Co., the Leeds Forge Co. and Brush Engineering. A number were also produced in France and Hungary. All coaches were painted 'Derby red', and they were all of steel construction. With a seating capacity of fifty-two, it weighed a little over 16 tons.

LER motor and control trailer, 1900.

then called Highgate. This involved the building of a connecting junction at Camden Town, which was to become a major feat of engineering.

Although customer numbers grew from 25 million in the first full year to 30 million in 1909, the line struggled to pay a dividend to shareholders due to the high construction costs. A pinch point was also identified at Charing Cross, where all trains terminated. In addition, this location did not have convenient connections with the Bakerloo and District lines. These problems were dealt with by running the line south a few hundred metres. Subsequently, in 1914 a clever addition to the line at the Strand was the completion of the previously mentioned single-loop line south, with just a single northbound platform at Charing Cross (Embankment), enabling a speedy turnaround of trains. Although this avoided the time involved in changing ends, it resulted in a 15-mph permanent speed restriction here, due to the sharp curvature of the loop. This is why the northbound platform is severely curved; it was part of the old loop. This was the line's first direct interchange for passengers at Embankment with the District and Bakerloo lines. It is also interesting to note that the Strand station name was first used on the Piccadilly line. Opened in 1907, it later became Aldwich.

The Charing Cross, Euston & Hampstead Railway tunnels were all of 12-foot diameter and, after a company name change in 1910, it was retitled the London Electric Railway Co. (LER). This came under the financial control of American tycoon Charles Tyson Yerkes, whose influence over the line was enormous. The first coaches came from America, built by the American Car Company. Contracts were also placed with the Leeds Forge Co. and Brush Electrical Engineering Co. A number were also built in France and Hungary. Constructed from steel, they weighed 16 tons 11 cwt. They were 50 feet 1.5 inches in length, 8 feet 7 inches in width and 9 feet 5 inches in height. The seating capacity was fifty-two, entrance being via gates sited at each end of the car.

David Lloyd George, then president of the Board of Trade, performed the opening ceremony on 22 June 1907. After the ceremony, the line was opened to the public, who were invited to travel free for the remainder of the day. 140,000 people took advantage of this. Yerkes had reason to congratulate himself. He had bought the powers for the construction of the line for £100,000 and, after that first day, he was convinced of the profits to be made. By mid-1910 well over 15,000 passengers a day were using the LER. On 1 July 1913 the financial control was passed over to the Underground Electric Railways Co. of London. This embraced all underground railways operating in London. The C&SLR had just celebrated the carrying of 10 million passengers in the first six months of operation that year.

The stations served at the time are of interest; the names as we know them today are in brackets. Starting from Embankment (Charing Cross, changed to Embankment again in 1978), Charing Cross (Strand, changed back to Charing Cross in 1978), Leicester Square, Oxford Street (Tottenham Court Road), Tottenham Court Road (Goodge Street), Euston Road (Warren Street), Euston, Mornington Crescent, and Camden Town. Going towards Highgate there was Kentish Town south, which was closed in 1924 due to lack of passengers, then Kentish Town, Tufnell Park and Highgate (Archway). Along the Golders Green branch were Chalk Farm, Belsize Park, Hampstead and Golders Green, which brought the line out into the open air and to its main depot and repair shops.

LER gate stock motor, with air-worked doors at Golders Green depot, 1910.

Golders Green 6b Standard Electric Door Stock Motor at depot, 1926.

The lack of an interchange at Euston between the LER and the C&SL Railways was still on the minds of both companies. The C&SLR station was in Eversholt Street, while the LER station was around the corner in Drummond Street. A more positive approach was made to correct this link; it was started prior to the outbreak of the First World War, but had to be halted when the war began, eventually being completed in 1922. The Underground Group had obtained powers to extend the C&SLR via the then-north and south sidings at Euston to link up at Camden Town, in order to give passengers a more direct route to Highgate and Golders Green – but this was to create a serious problem. Their tunnels were of a smaller bore and needed to be expanded in order to match those of the LER, so as to enable them to link up. Again the war prevented work starting and it wasn't until 1922 that the Moorgate–Euston section was completely closed down, in order that work to widen the tunnels could proceed quickly. Work was also commenced at night only south of Moorgate into 1923. Eventually the whole line was closed in order to speed up the work. The line was fully re-opened on 1 December 1924.

In the meantime, work was continuing south from Clapham Common in the new diameter tunnels. So too was work by the LER from Charing Cross (Strand) to Kennington, where another reversing loop, a total of 0.61 miles long from the centres of the south- and northbound platforms, was built. The Morden and Kennington extensions were completed in 1926, giving the world its longest tunnel at the time with a total of 16.5 miles.

Out in the open at Golders Green, work had been proceeding towards Hendon Central at a great pace, which opened in 1923. It had a scissors crossover south of the station, controlled by a small signal box sited at the northern end of the platform. When the extension to Edgware was completed, both the scissors crossover and the signal box were removed.

Progress north from here was in the building of a tunnel through Burrows Hill at Hendon to Colindale and on to Edgware, which was completed in 1924. Passing loops were provided at Brent, Hendon Central, Colindale and Burnt Oak to allow the limited express service running freedom through those stations. It is interesting to note that, in order to speed up the service to Edgware in 1926, alternate trains were to create confusion in that a train stopping at Colindale would bypass Burnt Oak, while a train bypassing Colindale would stop at Burnt Oak. That must have been a real headache for passengers wishing to get to both stations. The express service called at Golders Green, Hampstead and Camden Town, and then all stations to Kennington. There were no arrangements to repeated northbound since I have not discovered any documentation as such. It is not known when the passing loops were removed; historians state they were removed in 1936 but I recall as a child, when being taken into the West End in 1936, that the loops were still there then. I later discovered that Brent signal box was finally closed in January 1937. It is possible that during the vast scrap drives of late 1930s–1940s the passing loops may have been removed then.

In 1937, with both the City & South London Railway and the London Electric Railway now operating over the whole line, it was grouped under one name, the Northern line, which opened up new prospects regarding expansion. As early as 1935, plans were drawn up to extend the Highgate branch to East End (East Finchley) and onward over the lines operated then by the Great Northern Railway to Edgware and Barnet from King's Cross and Finsbury Park. Once again, work was started laying current rails into Barnet and Edgware (the Great Northern station). A new station was built at East End (East Finchley) and a new underground Highgate station beneath Highgate Hill.

Then came the Second World War, halting all work yet to be started, including the extension from Edgware to Bushey Heath and the Moorgate via Finsbury Park to Alexander Palace and Barnet plan. Work over the Barnet section was so far advanced that they were allowed to proceed and the first train to Barnet ran on 3 July 1939. The single line to Mill Hill, on the other hand, was not opened until 1941, due, it is believed, to its military sidings link. It was also intended that, during the off peak, half the city trains from Euston would divide at Finchley Central – half going to Edgware and half to Barnet. Naturally, it didn't happen. The double-tracking towards Edgware had advanced only to Hale Lane and this extra track was all removed, leaving just one single line, which at the time (1941) contained a long line of flat cars containing military Matilda Tanks from Mill Hill barracks. The Great Northern passenger service to Edgware had been withdrawn in 1940 and replaced by a bus service to Mill Hill East (240A). This bus service still operates today.

The King's Cross (LNER)–Barnet branch was first opened for passenger traffic in 1872; all the station buildings are of the common Great Northern Railways' gothic style. Only Finchley Central gained a refurbished Mill Hill–Barnet interchange platform, linked to the then-existing Barnet platform. Highgate station was the last incomplete station yet to open on this new line, although it was used as an air raid shelter during the war, where special trains, both morning and evening, made stops to drop off and pick up shelterers again. The final completion of the escalators saw the station finally opened later.

It's interesting to note that, in November 1936, the weekday rush-hour service consisted of ninety-four trains from Morden to Edgware and Highgate (Archway). In 1955, when the whole line to Barnet had been open for fifteen years, it totalled ninety-seven trains in the rush-hour service. As a lad at Golders Green, service trains available in 1948 totalled 100.

Two additional train depots were built; one was mainly intended for the proposed and never-completed extension to Finsbury Park and Alexander Palace (Highgate Woods). A steam service was still working over that branch until 1954, when it was withdrawn and the tracks on the branch were eventually taken up. Referring back to both depots on the Barnet branch, Barnet had eight new siding roads built. Being the highest station on the whole LT system, it was very open to the elements and the steep climb up from Totteridge to Barnet during icy weather could sometimes prove very difficult. The other depot was built at Highgate, adjacent to the woods sidings where a double-ended undercover depot gave stabling for ten trains, with two trains stabling on 25 road, the only siding out in the open. Special provision had to be made to stable a second train on 25 road. Highgate Woods, as I have already stated, was intended as a feed for the Alexander Palace branch. Here six trains were stabled at night. Only here was a ground shunter required, for the night shift only. These trains were withdrawn in December 1982 and Highgate Woods closed for stabling trains, at least as far as service trains were concerned.

Morden Standard Stock, awaiting departure on Open Day, 1924.

Morden Signal Box, 1955. The furthest drum sets up a train's platform number, the other the train's destination.

The opening of the Morden and Edgware extensions in 1926 saw the use of new all-electrically operated doors, heaters and seven-car trains. Some nine-cars were used but proved unsuccessful, since all stations only had platform room for seven cars. What is now known as the pre-1938 or standard stock had arrived, which had already proved very popular on other tube lines. In 1936 an experimental train made up of two cars was tested on the open section of the Piccadilly line. Streamlined, it was intended that they would reach speeds of 80 mph. They were unsuccessful. During the Second World War, two of these units were stabled on the disused sidings at Edgware, finally being removed during the early 1950s to Acton works where they were converted into trailer cars and returned to service. These were the forerunners of what we now know as the 1938 stock. From the day the first LER cars arrived, they were all painted Derby red, a practise still continued into the 1970s.

The only sign of the proposed extension to Bushey Heath from Edgware was the new signal box at Edgware, which I understand was built in 1938, and was never used until the automation plans arrived in the mid-1960s. It is now the machine room for said automation. The other remaining sign of this intended development is number 1 platform, which is still open to the elements.

Two station name changes took place during the 1940–76 period. Finchley (Church End) as it was known became Finchley Central. Under the Great Northern Railway's ownership, it was Finchley & Hendon. Brent on the Edgware section became Brent Cross in order to identify it with a new shopping development built in the early 1970s. The whole of the Northern line, alongside other underground lines, was eventually taken under the wing of London Transport Executive on 1 July 1933. In 1942 the line contained twenty-one signal cabins. During the Second World War, all of these were manned around the clock. Each had a set area of control. Five of these had signal-box boys – Finchley Central, Golders Green, Camden Town, Kennington and Morden.

Although some of the earlier C&SLR track layouts were similar, the operation of all signal cabins differed, mainly due to the amounts of traffic passing through their areas. Essentially it all came down to their general importance to the free flow of traffic and their capabilities in emergencies. All signal cabins had facilities for making a pot of tea. None of the tunnel boxes had running water – this had to be fetched from above for each shift. Neither were there toilet facilities. One had to call for a relief and travel to the surface for this. The boxes were very hot and dirty places to work through an eight-hour shift. Mosquitos infested many, and it wasn't uncommon for a signalman to get bitten on the eyelids, closing the affected eye. Soda was always available to get the swelling down.

The track diagrams illustrated in this book only cover the periods up to 1955. When automation started to entered the picture, a great many alterations were made to numerous layouts from 1955 onwards, mainly for simplicity and to keep maintenance costs down. All signalling is of the two-aspect colour-light system, save for the Barnet branch where illuminated disc type distant signals were also provided for the main line goods working that continued well into the late 1960s. They were eventually removed when this goods service from Finsbury Park was withdrawn.

On 1 January 1968, the then-Labour government gave its go ahead for a takeover of all LTE lines to the Great London Council who, with the help of the government, wiped out the then-£230 million capital debt, thus putting LTB on an even financial footing. At the time it was making an annual loss of £6 million a year, which included the operation of its vast bus fleet. LTB became London Transport Executive under the financial control of the GLC. Sir Richard Way, KCB, CBE, became the new Chairman of the Executive.

That's the brief history of the construction of what finally became the Northern line.

Chapter Two

My Personal Experience: From Manual to Automation

Leaving school aged fourteen in 1944 and applying for a position with London Transport Railways was to be my first disappointment. They replied informing me that they didn't take on juniors under fifteen and a half years of age. So an application was made to join the London Midland & Scottish Railway, which became my second choice and where I remained until London Transport contacted me for training in November 1946.

After a short period of training, I was dispatched to Hammersmith and City signal box, only to discover there was no such vacancy. There was a vacancy in the station's cloakroom, based on Great Western Railway practice, where I spend almost a year. It was from here that I was continually applying for signal-box vacancies.

In the late summer of 1947 I eventually gained a position as train recorder (box boy) at Kennington, the Northern line's busiest signal box. It was situated on the southern end of the northbound Charing Cross line. It was opened in 1929 after the earlier two City & South London signal boxes were closed after the completion and final link to the London Electric Railway (LER). It was a very small area in which two signalmen operated on each day shift, controlling north- and southbound traffic, and one on night shift. Unknown to me at the time, it was here I was to learnt my future trade. Learning how to record four trains travelling in two different directions every minute and a half was like being thrown to the wolves. I found both the job and the atmosphere exciting.

There were four lines to watch, two for the city lines and two for the Charing Cross lines. As a lad, I got to work with all of the signalmen during my two shifts. My job, as I've already mentioned, was to record every train movement. During the off-peak period I had write out the full service on foolscap sheets for the following day and as far in advance as possible. Usually the signalman operating the southbound traffic would take over the recording from me for this boring and laborious task. (When automation eventually arrived all these record sheets were printed for us). In signal boxes without lads, the shift signalman had to carry out this laborious task. It was at Kennington that I learnt the value of overhearing telephone conversations, since all messages were repeated back to the sender, which saved the signalman having to repeat it all to me, since messages mostly related to changes in the service order.

At Kennington and Camden Town, all the signalmen used the official timetable, making use of self-made lead pointers to keep track of where they were during the service. I spent eight months here until I obtained a similar vacancy at Golders Green signal box – out in the fresh air and much closer to home. It was here that was to become my real training ground. All three signalmen here were First World War veterans, each differing in character. One of them, over a weekend shift, showed me how to operate the signal frame (small levers). Gradually on his shift only I became more proficient, unbeknown to the remaining two signalmen until much later. During my thirty-two years, I was to meet a number of ex-box lads who learnt their trade in this way.

November 1949 was to become a year that was to involve me in ventures I didn't expect. This time it was National Service, which I served for two years, and three and a half years in the Territorial Army, which

Golders Green station, as viewed from the signal box in 1958.

Golders Green – the signalman's view south, 1955. In the far distance, the three tunnels can be seen. The one on the far left is just a short extension for the depot's shunt neck. The remaining pair are the service tunnels.

was then compulsory. Released from National Service in November 1951 and retraining again with London Transport, I was eventually appointed signalman at High Barnet. I had three weeks' training over all three shifts. This was to create a wide range of experiences here until I gained a position at a higher grade at Euston City signal box in the winter of 1952. That experience was to be a step back into the past for me. It was not a very hygienic position to be in. You soon discovered you were experiencing the very same as your predecessors in signal boxes deep underground just like this.

   In May 1953 I gained an appointment as relief signalman at almost twenty-two years of age. I looked forward to training for the wider variety of signal boxes, each, in their own way, offering moments of adrenaline and excitement. The down side to this appointment was that I had to cover my own vacancy until a new arrival was trained. So I remained there, covering the night shift during the Queen's coronation on 2 June 1953 for the special all-night service before my replacement arrived.

As relief signalmen we still had to cover Moorgate and Drayton Park signal boxes on the Northern and City line. Since there were no night shifts at either, both were to be very early start shifts. A porter signalman covered the middle shifts at both signal cabins. At the time I was living in Acton in west London, which had an all-night bus service with good connections in Central London for both signal boxes.

Just prior to the mid-1950s, there were rumblings of automating the entire line. Naturally older members of staff shrugged it off as impossible and something that would never happen, it being too complicated, but it did. Camden Town's signal box was revamped on 23 July 1955 and, while this revamping was progressing, Camden Town's controls were transferred onto a small room on the abandoned pre-1924 Barnet platform.

Eventually all was replaced in the same spot that the old lever frame once resided. It had been replaced with a small desk containing just push buttons on 17 September 1955. The biggest advancement in modern technology was that the signalman got to sit down while operating the desk. Eyebrows were raised even more when a test programme machine roll was linked into the southbound Charing Cross trailing junction in September 1957, containing the entire timetable for that area. This was on a type of piano roll containing thirty punch holes. This was to make this junction a first come, first served situation from both the southbound

Camden Town temporary signal box diagram, 1956.

feeds and from both the Barnet and Edgware branches. This was to create a little confusion in the rush hour. This had become the test bed for later programme machine operations.

Operating a signal box, particularly those in the open section, was interesting because they all had their own distinct sounds and their own particular peculiarities. No two signalmen operated their boxes in the same way. Each was an individual in his own right and his judgement differed from any of his colleagues, although each would keep clearly to the rules laid down by the general rulebook. I was always told when being taught in my first box that one can bend a rule without actually breaking it. This became very clear over the years, looking back, as many of us got away with some very clever train moves not generally recognised, but in complete safety.

I've spent hours searching my mind over the varying layouts and the mixture of moves not associated with the movement of passengers. A study of the accompanying diagrams will help the reader understand many of them and why they were made. Having a line split into two sections will make it difficult, but I'll commence with Edgware and work to Camden Town, then up to Barnet. The signal box codes (in brackets) were all changed after 2013. Those shown are the original area codes as affixed to signals.

Edgware (AE)

Edgware originally had two platforms. A third platform was added in 1932 as an island platform in connection with a proposed extension to Bushy Heath. Nos 2 and 3 were totally under cover while No. 1, the only remaining part of the original island platform, is open to the elements.

When I first trained for this signal box, the numbering of the platform starting signals confused me. No. 1 starter was numbered 33, No. 2 was 32 and No. 3 platform was 31. Yes, many a wrong signal lowered there. Unlike other areas, all the points and signals were operated electrically (as was Colindale) and one would hear the whine of point motors and the slight thump of train stops going down; each had its own distinct sound. It was also the only station to have de-railers fitted to the track. They

Edgware signal box, 1956, built in 1923 to handle traffic with just two platforms. An additional platform was added in 1938 in readiness for the proposed extension to Bushy that was cancelled.

Edgware interlocking lever frame, now sited in the new signal box, 2012. (Tony Cook)

were a large cast-iron block, shaped like half of a cottage loaf; it rested on one running rail, being lowered when the points were reset set to normal. There were three at Edgware; one at the end of No. 1 platform, one in

Edgware programme room, the electronic brain that talks to other brains down the line, 2012. (Tony Cook)

16 siding and one at the outlet from the depot. The depot housed fourteen trains and had a double-shunt neck; the second was removed in 1985. The intended 1939 route change tracks for south main traffic remained until finally removed in the 2000s.

Entrance to the depot can only be made from either No. 2 or 3 platforms, although there was a shunt move one could make from No. 1 platform south to reverse back into No. 2 or 3, and then to depot. This move was carried out every Sunday morning when the train stabled on 16 siding was switched for a clean train in preparation for the Monday service. Automation, when it arrived, removed this arrangement and the siding. A handy route was from No. 2 platform over No. 7 points south when bringing a train in service from depot to No. 3 platform. There was no route indicator above No. 32 signal to this effect and in the 1950s many drivers made emergency stops when they didn't swing over at the first crossover, irrespective of the train running into the opposite platform.

In 1936 dividing a seven-car train into two trains was introduced for a short time for the same reasons I have explained here. In those days it was done by pole, having first disconnected the electrics and the air hose before dividing a train. Uncoupling a train in the early 1950s was much simpler and completely mechanical where both parts formed two separate trains, just as it was in 1936, and it was to become a real headache. All was fine when the service was running to time; if there had there been an incident during the rush hour – and there was hardly a day went by that something didn't happen to disrupt the service – then you really began to work. Printed at the top of the driver's outer front cab door is a letter A or D. (In 1929 it was A and B for the new air-worked door trains.)

All stock for uncoupling should be 'A' north and one would study the trains going south prior to their uncoupling trip as to which way round they were then. Remember, there was a loop at Kennington and should a train be the wrong way round then it would have to be routed via Kennington siding to keep it the right way round. It sounds simple, doesn't it, but not when you're a busy signalman at Kennington and, in the chaos around you, if you forget about these unbooked moves, then Edgware and Barnet had a problem. As far as I recall, uncoupling took place at Morden, Edgware, High Barnet and also just one train at Finchley Central for the Sunday Mill Hill East shuttle service. I will write more on uncoupling later.

Edgware looking south, showing 16 siding in 1956. This was eventually removed when automation arrived.

Edgware signal box, 1956. The depot's car examiner in view.

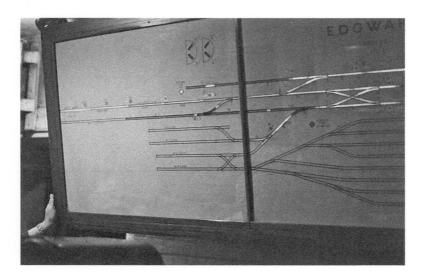

Edgware diagram, 1956. Note the depot had two shunt necks. The upper two of the four were hardly ever used.

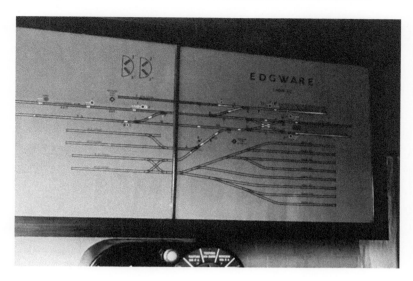

Edgware signal box diagram 1b, 1956.

Edgware signal box lever frame, 1956.

Colindale (AC)

Famous for its air pageants held at the old fighter station at Hendon Airfield, Colindale is now a housing estate (although it is the nearest station for the new RAF museum). In the Blitz of the Second World War, Colindale station received a direct hit during a raid. The station was partly rebuilt but the booking office was nothing more than a wooden shed until the top station was rebuilt in the 1960s. Essentially, Colindale was a time-checking point, since it was mostly in automatic working during the rush hour. A number of trains were reversed here during the rush hour in order to relieve workings at Edgware and to provide an empty train for passengers at Hendon and Brent. It's never been confirmed that there was a southbound passing loop here at all, due to restricted space at the sidings southbound outlet.

A trainee brought to my attention a peculiarity I wasn't aware of at that time. While talking to the driver of a reversing train, he pointed out the signal was clear for him to go but there was still a train in the siding. Obtaining a release all was put right, but this particular guy would keep

Colindale northbound starter and disc 1, 1956. We were not to know that signals such as this all over the line would disappear completely in 2014.

Colindale during an early shift, with myself at the controls, 1956.

Colindale passing trains, 1955, with one train heading to Edgware, and another about to pass south. Not a good shot but you are able to see the reversing siding.

Colindale diagram, 1954. Out of the rush hour in automatic operation – it only reversed trains during the morning and evening peak service.

Colindale lever frame, 1954.

trying to put two trains in the siding. (This was something left over from the uncoupling days of 1929 I believe). Interestingly he had brought to light a safety matter that I hadn't been aware of before.

Colindale was also the site of the ever-boiling kettle and was a favourite spot for crews to leave their respective tea cans with little notes attached, informing me when they would be around again. These would be lined up in set order on the windowsill until their set time arrived. When the signal box closed under the automation programme, a special arrangement was made where crews could make tea from a large hot-water urn situated under the passenger stairs. These brief contacts with train crews were to pay off later in my career where a favour was required in return, such as when their help was really needed for a quick shunt somewhere. Early in December 1982, all Colindale reversing trains ceased and were sent to Edgware, thus offering a better and more frequent service from there to the city.

Golders Green

This was one of my favourite signal boxes. The vast variety of routes one could set up in the course of a shift was a way to speed a shift through. A three-route station, very little has changed since its original opening, save for the removal of the crossover just south of platform 5, which allowed northbound trains to run directly into the southbound platform. A pity, I could have used that route many times over the years.

A highly complicated signal box as far as interlocking was concerned, I was always at ease here. When automation arrived, all interlocking was divided between two machine rooms – one for northbound traffic and one for the southbound traffic, but connected electronically regarding interlocking. There was always one rule that prevailed here during the morning rush hour service: all southbound city trains had to be worked through the middle route, thus easing the crowds on the platform. This wasn't always the case, since many relief signalmen and some relief station masters hated this. Even under later automation, a great many city trains were routed through the middle route.

There were a number of get-out moves here. By get-out, I mean a Golders Green terminating train wrongly directed in the northbound platform could be shunted north and back into the middle or, if it was running really late, it could be worked directly south from here. The northbound loop was a holding route, particularly when the service became disorganised. From here a signalman could see the number of the train, thus it would get routed correctly, either to Edgware or reversed at Golders Green.

One of the riskiest routes to set up during the daylight hours was what we termed a main line shunt. This was a shunt from either of the three platforms southbound, stopping about five coaches inside the tunnel and

Golders Green temporary diagram, 1958. It would be thirteen years before Golders Green would be transferred to Cobourg Street control room.

Golders Green automation cable bridge, constructed in 1971 to link two IMRs. (Tony Cook)

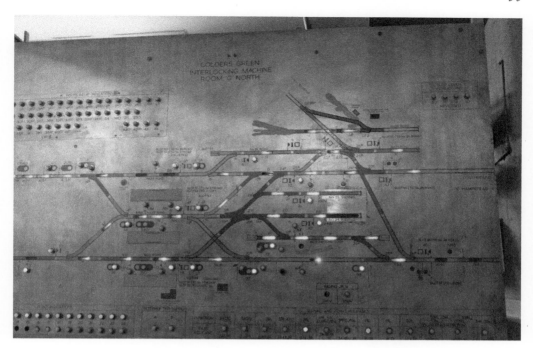

Golders Green northbound IMR diagram, sited in a new building in 1971. (Tony Cook)

Golders Green northbound IMR lever frame. (Tony Cook)

Golders Green northbound IMR programme memory brains. (Tony Cook)

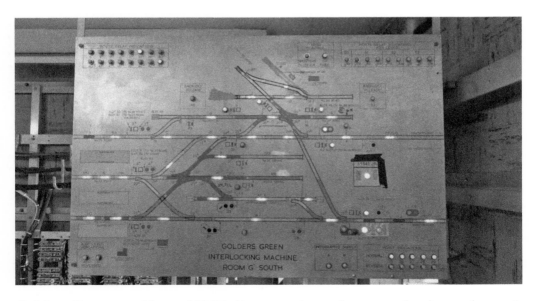

Golders Green southbound IMR diagram, situated next to the depot shunter's cabin. (Tony Cook)

Golders Green southbound IMR lever frame. Both north and south IMRs are linked. (Tony Cook)

Golders Green southbound IMR relays. The electronic side of all interlocking. (Tony Cook)

reversing back, either to another platform or to depot. This was used mainly to get trains quickly to depot, particularly very late at night when the normal shunt neck was already occupied. Unfortunately, in daylight hours, going from bright sunlight into pitch black during such a move, the stopping-point marker in the tunnel was missed. During the dark hours, this wasn't a problem. As a box boy here we lost a train like this for ten minutes, then it re-appeared. There is no way a signalman would let another train proceed until one was able to ascertain where the intended shunt train had gone. During my relief signalman days this happened to me, with the crew eventually ringing from Hampstead. In this case it was an extra trip to Euston siding and back for them. Years later this stopping point was illuminated.

Later signalmen still feared this move but some of the diehards in the later regulating control room still made it. It was always wise to have such a train double-ended both for safety and a fast shunt to depot. Everyone at some time tried to get three trains moving south at once – it was the local party trick. No. 1 northbound to 24 siding, then middle road to south route and No. 3 road to depot via 26 road. This could also be achieved in the opposite direction and used to scare the pants off unsuspecting drivers.

In the case of a serious incident on the line, and there were many, the cry went out to stable as many trains as you could. Every available means was taken to get trains out of the way and one would stable out in the sidings first in the hope that things will normalise. This was done in order to leave the middle free for a following Golders Green train that was on time. Leaving a train sitting in the northbound loop was a crime. Get it into number 1 platform and back out.

There was always an unwritten rule that passengers must not be carried through shunt routes, mainly due to the lack of safe main line type points interlocking. On a number of occasions I have had to do this in order to keep trains moving. Routing a train full of passengers across the main from Hampstead into 26 road and back into No. 3 road was a favourite when nothing could be routed to Edgware. While it is possible to route trains from all platforms south, No. 3 platform road was impossible to fill without a time-wasting shunt. Having to make decisions such as this involved one in all sorts. Firstly the driver would ring up and question the signal, then you would have to advise the station master, then the line controller, without telling him how you were able to make a train available. He would have his hands too full to even worry about it. The whole idea was to get as many trains back as soon as possible. During very late running, one would have a train detrain at Hampstead and run it into 26 road empty, change ends and finally reverse back out southbound. Stabling trains directly to depot from the northbound route meant detraining at Hampstead as booked and then proceeding across from the tunnel at Golders Green directly into depot. After so many years of this timetabled practice, it all ceased in August 1997. I was always being asked where the third tunnel went to – well, I can tell you: about a half a car. It was extended in 1923 to accept longer trains. This is the main depot's shunt neck and will just hold a seven-car train with just half a car in said tunnel, as already mentioned.

One Saturday night, 14 October 1961, the power frame was ripped out and replaced by a push-button desk, all completed in less than seven hours. This included all telephone links that now became switch keys, a great advance on the old magneto-type handset we had, which had been there since the line first opened. Hampstead had been added earlier in December 1958, its controls contained in a metal box affixed to the end of the power frame. Now it was all contained in sliding drawers on a new desk. On 31 January 1965 Edgware control was transferred to Golders Green. A month later, Colindale was added. This section was mounted on a wooden box, something very like an arcade game, complete with each areas control buttons. It remained like this for six years. Carrying out reformations to the service at both Golders Green and Edgware at the same time, and during interruptions to the service, was both stressful and tiring for this singly manned desk. Passing on all these changes to the control centre at Leicester Square and the line controller required restraint and mental control. These operations usually meant the staff in the control room at Leicester Square having to manually operate for long periods, always in a standing position due to the positioning of the push buttons set high up, since the programme machines became useless when the service was so disruptive.

Finally, on the night of 13 March 1971, all controls were transferred from Golders Green to Cobourg Street, Euston. Automation had been advanced. Just keep in mind that all I have related about Golders Green was about to become automated, this covering all the routes I have mentioned.

Golders Green northbound approach, 1955. Being able to see your trains was invaluable when the service was disorganised. Camden Town missed out-of-turn movements. It was here that they were corrected. Note the 'A' above the cab.

Golders Green northbound train, about to leave the tunnel in 1957. The first set of points is the route directly to depot. The second set is the route into the loop. The two trains in view are stabled in the two outside sidings.

Golders Green City middle road. In 1955 it was used to terminate the Morden via City service during the off peak. In the rush hour, it became a bi-directional route for both southbound and northbound traffic.

Golders Green depot, the view south from the depot's lighting tower. It was 1963 and construction for the south interlocking machine room was already underway next to the depot shunter's cabin.

Golders Green depot
turntable, 1963. Not
what you expect to see.
It was installed in 1900,
but is now filled in – a
small piece of local
Underground history.

Golders Green depot
in 1963 – the second
largest depot on the line.
Taken from the depot's
lighting tower.

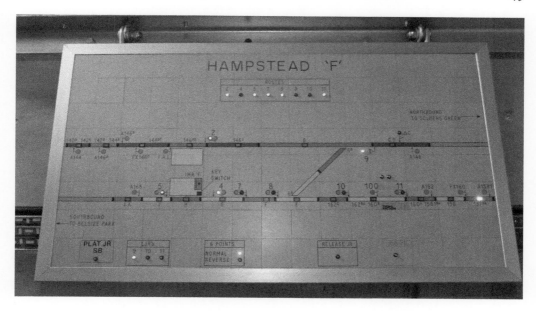

Hampstead IMR Diagram. (Tony Cook)

Hampstead (F)

Containing a single crossover that could reverse trains in either direction, Hampstead was basically an emergency point. The signal box was sited at the north end of the southbound platform. I manned this box on odd nights for works train operations and a whole week on early shift when Golders Green was being modernised, just in case things didn't go according to plan. The deepest station on the Underground, there was an emergency exit via spiral stairs. There were 365 stairs to climb to the surface. I did this just once.

Camden Town (E)

This was one of the last signal cabins for which I qualified, with the new desk and not the old lever frame, although I visited socially at the old signal box a number of times on my spare shift days. It was a 24-hour signal box containing two men per shift, one on the night shift with a middle shift during the day.

The signal box was situated at the south end of the Barnet northbound platform. The power frame was sited in a position aligned with the flow of traffic. Behind them was a large window that drew interested onlookers to it during traffic. It was bricked up when the new desk was eventually installed. On 13 June 1955 the controls were transferred into a small room next to a ventilation shaft situated between the old and new Highgate platforms. There are still the original LER platforms about 3 feet lower than the existing platforms. I never did discover if the same applied to all the old workings, since most of the old passages were sealed up.

It was on the temporary controls that I learnt the layout for Camden Town. The controls were not quite what I was used to and I learnt the hard way. What a mad house that was. Finally, after almost two months of covering shifts in this hellhole, it was all transferred back into the old signal box site, which had been completely refurbished. It now had tiles and a new red tiled floor. The new control desk now had Mornington Crescent added to it. The big problem was that the diagram was now facing the flow of traffic, which took some getting used to. (Remember what I mentioned about sounds – now they came from different directions from what you were used to).

It was now a three-man signal box, which was one man per shift. The station inspectors carried out the meal reliefs for a short period. It was at Camden Town, on 24 September 1957, that the first programme machine was tested prior to its wider general use. The machine contains a roll of Melinex, in which thirty holes have been punched that contained encoded timetable information; this data is read by electrical contacts. The programme machine was the brainchild of Mr Robert Dell OBE, then London Transport's head signal engineer.

Basically the whole service was typed out on a continuous Melinex plastic roll, where each section of the timetable for this route ran both southbound branches from both Barnet and Edgware for the service via Charing Cross. The continuous roll contained the thirty punch-holes I've just mentioned, like a pianola roll you see at fairgrounds. It was into the punch holes that the slim metal fingers dropped. Should the fingers' circuit set up not agree with the next train's arrival, a single-stroke warning would sound informing the signalman it was about to dispatch the train out of order. Failing to prevent this happening, he would let it ride, making a note to pass on the change to Kennington control, which was now based at Leicester Square (from Jan 1958). This test machine controlling the southbound CX junction now made it completely automatic. Since this south junction only contained trailing points, no mechanical operation was required; the only problem was that the first train to reach a certain point on the track would automatically get the route unless halted. This created many problems if one was distracted by a phone call, etc. – it passed on these problems to Kennington, since a large number of trains from Barnet terminated at Kennington, as did the Edgware service. Some of these trains returned to the different destinations from whence they came. There was no way Kennington could define which train was which. (Hence the staff number checking assistance). Acting on information of any reversed working of trains, a great many returned to Camden Town undetected and, providing the drivers stopped at a junction signal and questioned the route by telephone (a great many did not), the correct route would be given. Yes, they were exciting days – completely crazy, when one looks back on those times.

Finally in the summer of 1958, all Camden Town's controls were transferred to Leicester Square control room. Only two of the original signalmen went with the transfer. During the old lever frame days, it was always claimed Camden Town was the fastest junction on the line. They overlooked Euston's reversing service during the rush hour, which made

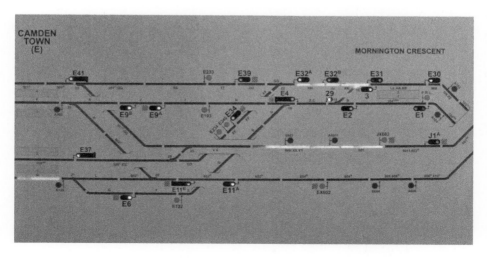

Camden Town, taken from the Cobourg Street control room to show what an engineering feat this really was in 1924. (Tony Cook)

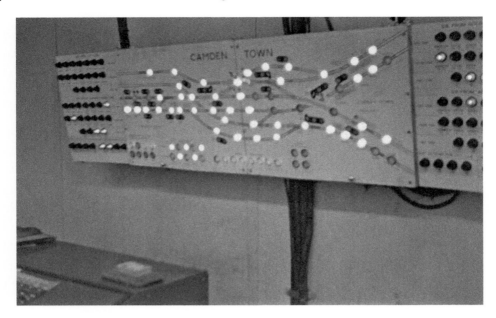

The author at Camden Town desk, 1956. When this was taken, the programme machine test had not been installed. That took place in 1957, where the table is on the left.

Camden Town temporary signal box diagram, 1956.

Camden Town northbound diagram in the interlocking machine room. Photograph taken in 2012. (Tony Cook)

Camden Town northbound machine room interlocking lever frame at 2012. (Tony Cook)

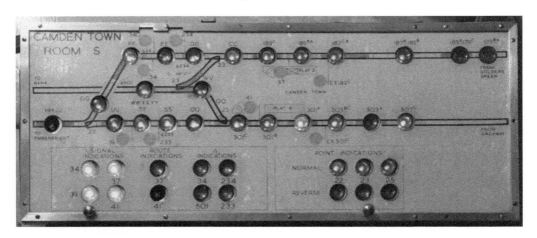

Camden Town southbound machine room diagram in 2012. Just looking at this half section makes it look so simple. Add this to the northbound section and it becomes a strain.

Camden Town southbound machine room interlocking lever frame, hidden away from prying eyes. This was just a small part of this busy junction.

Kennington the fastest. Mind you, credit where credit's due, Camden Town had the most trains moving at any one time, which sort of makes them the fastest.

Camden Town. This was the original test programme machine for the trailing southbound Charing Cross junction. It did have problems in running away. It was soon rectified. When all the controls were moved to Leicester Square in June 1958, only two of the original signalmen went with it all.

Now we move to the start of the Barnet branch, where we shall continue on down to Camden Town again, taking in on the way the operations of the four signal boxes on the Barnet branch.

High Barnet (NU)

This was my first signal box back in 1951, one that had the company of the signal lineman, whose separate room adjoined the signal box. The steep climb from Totteridge to Barnet must have been quite something in the old steam days. As it was, snow and ice were the problems faced by tube trains trying to reach the highest point on the Underground in really icy weather. Barnet had three platforms and a depot, with stabling for eight trains. One would think the peaceful outlook was ideal – not so. Prior to each rush hour, the trains starting from depot would already have a train tested and checked, called a Target Train. This was used should one of the trains develop a fault. It was bad practise to clear the route for the next train from depot as soon as the previous train had cleared. Should the next train become cancelled through no crew being available or mechanical failure? The crew would switch to the target train while you obtained an interlocking release, all time consuming.

High Barnet signal box diagram 1951.

High Barnet siding in
the winter of 1951.

High Barnet signal box
lever frame 1951.

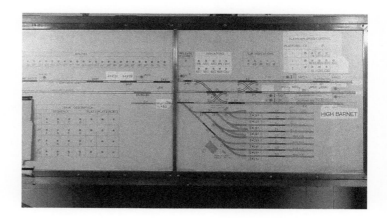

High Barnet new
diagram, 2014. (Tony
Cook)

High Barnet station and sidings 1951.

High Barnet; new building in the old goods yard and the sidings 2014. (Tony Cook)

High Barnet programme machines, 2012 – no more Melinex. Minimised electronics take over.

While covering a rest day at Barnet, I had the unfortunate experience of seeing a train depart from the siding without a signal being cleared and there was nothing I could do to prevent it. I watched as the first five cars swung and slewed across the tracks, bending current rails as though they were made of rubber. The rust shaken out from such force completely covered the train. Naturally my immediate concern was for the crew. It seems the regular signalman had always been clearing the signal for this train early. Thinking it was the same this day, the driver decided to drive said train from the opposite end and derailed his train since the route had not been set. Both members of the crew were shocked but unhurt. Both sat in the signal cabin to await the arrival of officials. The siding was fully operational for the evening stabling.

Right up to October 1962, when it was finally withdrawn, a daily goods train worked into Barnet six days a week. Timetabled as 2512, it used to arrive during the back end of any late morning rush hour, running via its only route, into the goods yard via No. 1 platform. It wasn't unknown to see it sail into No. 3 platform through misinformation. That meant a shunt into the depot neck and back into No 1. Fortunately the accompanying shunter, being a very competent man, piloted the train through the whole route. It wasn't until some years later that it was discovered he was colour blind and had taught himself which was red and which was green.

A heavy fall of rain caused a landslip on the northbound road into Barnet that gave some concern during 1956. In 1969 the ninety-seven-year-old bridge across the Great North Road was replaced during that summer at a cost of £200,000. Part of the cost was met by the GLC who, with plans to widen the road, caused LT to lift the tracks a further 2 feet and 6 inches in order to comply with the Ministry of Transport's standard 16 feet and 6 inches of headroom for road traffic. The new bridge now has a span of 71 feet.

With the introduction of automation, a great many alterations were made. One of these was the cancellation of uncoupling moves in all platforms and in the depot. Others included the introduction of a driver's plunger sited at all shunt signals in the depot, together with an illuminated indicator situated at the head of the depot, which displayed the number of the next train due from depot. This was all controlled by programme machine.

Barnet control was transferred to Cobourg Street on 12 September 1971. The introduction of programme machines solved the problem with the platform signs, always a sore point with passengers. Under programme machine operation, once a signal was cleared for a train in the platform, the description for that train was switched out and only showed the next train from that platform when the first train had departed, a great advance from the old manual days.

Finchley Central (NQ)

Retaining most of its earlier main-line characteristics up until 1964, the get-out moves gave a great deal of variety in operating the signal box. Unfortunately, automation saw the removal of a number of shunt moves that got us out of trouble in the past. In those early days under LT, it was possible to shunt a Mill Hill train back into the south siding or reverse a

Barnet train from the Barnet platform back south or into the south siding. There is a north siding used for reversing booked terminating trains and, on a Sunday, an empty train from Highgate depot used to shunt into the south siding, uncouple, and form the two trains required for the Mill Hill shuttle service. The last journey on a Sunday night involved complicated shunt moves in order to get the two trains re-coupled and back to Highgate depot.

I mentioned the goods workings earlier. Finchley Central took the brunt of all this working, which was mainly coal for the gas works at Mill Hill. Just for interest's sake, I'll list the goods working:

2520 worked Wellington sidings at Highgate, East Finchley yard, Finchley Central and Mill Hill Military yard.
2512 worked Woodside Park, Totteridge and High Barnet.
2518 worked Mill Hill yard, later taken over by 2520.
2514, 2524 and 2528 were all Mill Hill gas trains.
2526 worked Edgware but was withdrawn late in 1964.

It was a rule that no more than nineteen wagons, including the brake van, were to work over the tube lines, but on a Monday morning it was nothing to see over sixty empties coming out of Mill Hill gas yard, since the

Finchley Central, approaching north, 1956. Just passing the under the wall siding for stabling goods wagons.

Finchley southbound to siding, 1958. This reveals points removed with automation.

Finchley Central diagram, 1956. Here you can view original point work, later removed. The route from the northbound Barnet platform to south and the south siding to Mill Hill platform are no more.

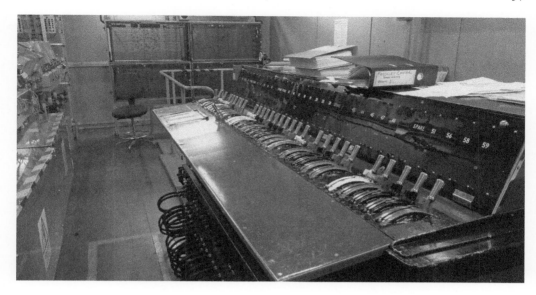

Finchley Central interlocking machine room lever frame in 2012. Greatly reduced, but still sited in the old signal box. (Tony Cook)

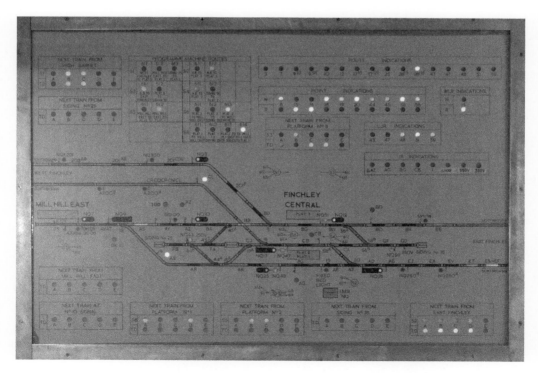

Finchley Central interlocking machine room diagram in 2012. (Tony Cook)

Saturday and Sunday trains always returned to King's Cross light engine, leaving their loads to be emptied over the weekend. Many attempts were made to stop these long trains, without success, and they were always a grand sight as they struggled uphill all the way to East Finchley at 40 mph or more. The rule appertaining to one train down the single line to Mill Hill at any one time was amusing, to say the least. While in practise it was carried out to the letter where tube trains were concerned, one would send down the Edgware goods, then a gas train, then one for Mill Hill military yard. Add a passenger train to that and you now have four trains on a single line. It was quite safe since each train was protected by a ground frame that in turn was locked by a passenger train being in the platform at Mill Hill. Once the passenger train had left the single line, there was nothing to stop the signalman from letting all three goods trains out, but one at a time.

Staying with goods traffic, there were rare occasions when a special goods train would be worked to Finchley Central on a weekend. This would be shunted into a siding sited to the left of the northbound road (known as under the wall), just south of the station, where the engine was uncoupled and returned to King's Cross loco via the northbound Barnet platform and reversed back south. The remaining train would be moved by 2520 when it arrived the following day. This siding was removed in the early 1970s. On 15 October 1967, control was transferred into a temporary signal box while work was carried out installing programme machines in the old signal box.

One thing always stuck in my mind about Finchley Central, which was the amount of leg mileage one covered during a shift. To give you some idea: to set a route for a Barnet train from East Finchley involved No. 16 points, No. 20 points, and signals 17, 28 & 29. Having replaced these after a Barnet train's passage, one set up for a Mill Hill that involved Nos 49 and 60 points and signals 25, 28 and 29. To bring a train up from Mill Hill, one required signals 37, 9 and 12, having first replaced 8 and 49 points and 3, 17 and 12 signals. Speed these moves up in your head and it will give you some idea of the movements made during the rush hour, not counting timetabled reversing moves that would also be taking place. Control was finally transferred to Cobourg Street on 14 December 1969. There were to be no more steam-train movements.

East Finchley (NP)

Controlling the junction to Park Junction and Highgate depot, East Finchley was basically another timing point. The goods workings added some interest. There have been occasions where, with the assistance of another crew, a train could be reversed north to south via 23 points just north of the station. This was done with empty stock transfers.

Later, new trainees at Cobourg Street were asked to study the line and tell us where they would get a fourteen-car train off the line. We used to get some amusing answers; basically should this happen, and it did, a number of times, at Golders Green northbound for instance, it would go directly across to the depot. The sensible thing in this situation was to have the driver on the north end drive the train backwards behind the shunt signal, since a driver at the southern end wouldn't know where to stop. This was also applied at East Finchley, since 23 point was also the exit route from the goods yard and north to Finchley Central. As a second choice, one would send the train just south of No. 9 signal on the Mill Hill single line and back to Highgate depot, again with a driver at each end. Obviously, in all cases it would depend on which end of the train was faulty. One was unable to make use of sidings since there were very few, and with only a maximum of a nine-car train length.

The author at East Finchley signal box, 1955.

East Finchley diagram and lever frame in 2012. Now air-operated. (Tony Cook)

East Finchley junction, view north in 2012. (Tony Cook)

East Finchley to Highgate depot and Woods sidings plungers. (Tony Cook)

Park Junction (NH) (Highgate)

Park Junction was the largest signal box on the Northern line, with over 40 per cent of its levers wasted. Had the proposed 1935 modernisation plans been carried out, this would have been an interesting signal box. As it was, it became a white elephant. Essentially, there would have been two fans for the depot, one for Barnet and one for the Moorgate via Finsbury Park service. The additional stabling point later became Highgate Woods, where five trains were stabled each night. Here a ground shunter was required, since all the points, with the exception of the feed-in route points, were all hand-worked in the Woods sidings. It was also from here that some works trains operated. All stock transferers from the then-Northern–City line brought in here by steam train from Finsbury Park. A total of ten trains were stabled in Highgate depot, two of them on 25 road, which required special arrangements since it was not possible to give signals to a train onto a road already occupied. Eight of the roads were completely covered and access was available from both ends of the depot, as already explained. I only had cause to use the south end once, when one of the trains on 25 road was due out before the one on the north end. The clouds

Park Junction signal box interior, 1955. The largest on the line.

Park Junction Wellington sidings and depot, 1953.

Park Junction Highgate tunnels, 1955. The points in the foreground were to the Alexandra Palace branch.

Park Junction south. Alexandra Palace branch on the left. The north crossing leads into Highgate Woods sidings and the south end of the depot, 1955.

of rust shaken from this (hardly ever used) route gave some concern but all was well.

The little-used point work eventually came into disuse and I believe has now been removed completely and, instead, new extensions laid to double the stabling capacity here when PTI automation arrived.

When I trained for this signal box in 1954, a steam service still operated to Alexander Palace, where block codes were used but no block instrument like those used in main-line signal boxes. The Old Great Northern always insisted bell codes still be used over the Barnet branch for empty trains and all goods trains even though, as I have already mentioned, no real block instruments existed in either East Finchley or Finchley Central, just a Morse-type key. Just four trains were stabled in Highgate depot each day after the morning peak, to return for the evening peak. Saturdays sometimes saw two or three engines coupled, sent from Finsbury to Park Junction to give the signalman at Finsbury No. 7 signal box some breathing space. They were reversed and sent back; these moments were rare. This was to be the only box not to have been affected immediately by automation (up to 1979). It really was a site of wasted manpower and one always took a good book when covering this signal box.

This was the only signal box on the Northern line that was never controlled from Cobourg Street control room under the automation programme. Nor were programme machines ever installed here. Later, the new-type programme machines were linked to the depot service only.

Archway (NN)

This was the one-time terminus of the LER, prior to the 1940 extension to Barnet. It had an interesting layout. The signal box was sited at the south end of the southbound platform.

It was extremely handy in reversing trains in an emergency via a scissors southbound crossover, which enabled one to reverse back from both the southbound and the northbound platforms and back south. When the extension went forward, the north-to-south platform crossover was removed, leaving just the north platform to south crossover. One had to place the starting signal at Tufnell Park at danger, before a following train arrived that would prevent you from doing so due to the very tight

Archway signal box sited on the south end of the southbound platform. Originally, as seen here, it controlled a north-to-south crossover and a siding. The crossover was removed in the late 1950s, when automation took control.

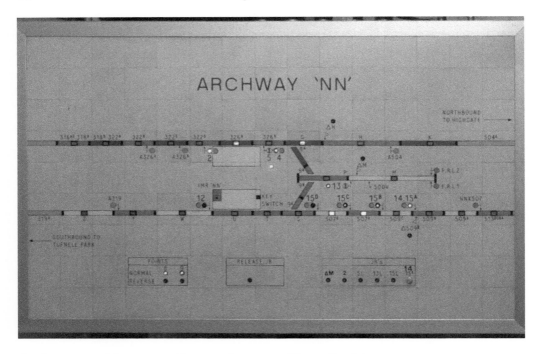

Archway machine room diagram in 2012. (Tony Cook)

Archway IMR interlocking frame, sited in the old signal box 2012. (Tony Cook)

interlocking here. There was also a siding north of the station; this is all that survives today after the complete removal of the crossover in 1967. In its heyday, a great deal of reversing was carried out here, particularly in the winter when a failure out in the open section, due to snow or serious mechanical failures, etc., would throw the load onto Archway. In 1952 this was still a porter signalman's position.

The signal boxes along the City route are:

Euston (City) (J)

I always thought it strange that the old City & South London Railway made use of island platforms at their terminating points, such as Euston, Angel, Stockwell and Clapham Common. Mind you, they only ran three-car trains in those days, plus the loco. The long line shut down when the tunnels were increased from 10 to 12 feet in diameter, in order to meet the running standards of the LER prior to the eventual link-up in 1924 at Camden Town. Euston was to see many changes over the following years. The remaining island stations were to change in the twenty-first century.

All the signal box had under its control was a scissors crossover and a siding that were both south of the station on the northbound route. Reversing was made from either platform, as well as from south to north via a shunt movement. It was also the route for works trains to Lille Bridge depot on the District line via King's Cross loop, which was the link to the eastbound Piccadilly line. Since it was not possible to give signals for this route in reverse, the inspector at King's Cross would walk through the tunnel with a 'wrong line' order, which, after securing the points at King's Cross, would ride through with the train to a point just north of the loop where it would continue under signals, previously set, onto the Piccadilly line. Should there be two such trains, the inspector would carry two wrong line orders, giving the second to the signalman at Euston. Upon hearing the first train was clear, the signalman would hand it to the second driver, who would then proceed. There was an east-to-west single crossover west of the station, which was used to reverse works trains. It was also used to reverse empty passenger trains for Acton works until it was halted and trains were dispatched to Arnos Grove to reverse.

Euston City signal box, 1953. This was a real eye-opener. The conditions were terrible. Nothing had been changed in more than sixty years of its existence. The two boxes at each end indicated to the signalman the destinations of trains approaching.

Euston and its temporary diagram in November 1958, long before the track changes were implemented.

Euston City machine room, 2012. (Tony Cook)

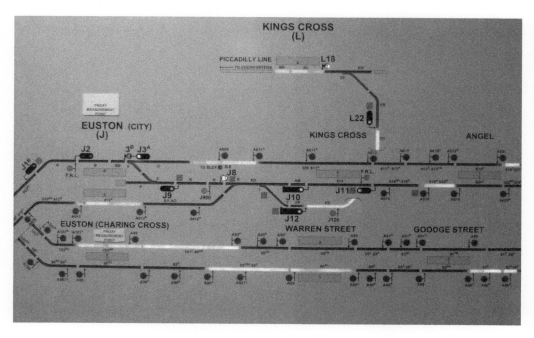

Euston and King's Cross diagram at Cobourg Street control room, 2014. (Tony Cook)

Euston City new IMR Diagram 1, 2014. (Tony Cook)

The monotony of the rush-hour service was broken during the afternoon service when four trains were reversed north to south via the southbound platform. Here, use was made of what we termed as a step-up crew. The first crew would leave the train; that driver then operated a plunger to indicate he was clear of his cab; and the signal for southbound movement would clear. This would normally take one-and-a-half minutes. So many drivers forgot to operate the plunger and one would hear the signalman shout, 'Plunger', and the plunger operated before the train could proceed. A one-to-one reversing service was carried out during the off-peak periods here. Three-car units that reversed at Euston did so in the northbound platform. No plunger was required here since they had a four-minute turnaround period and a plunger was not included for northbound reversing trains. This ceased when automation took over. This saw the removal of the shunt move north and the north-to-south section of the crossover. One good thing that came out of this was that it was now made possible to route works trains directly into the King's Cross loop.

The rebuilding of the mainline station saw the removal of the lifts and escalators installed; this was a vast improvement to the large flow of passengers, particularly at holiday time. It might be of interest to point out that the old Euston LER exit was at the south end of the Charing Cross platform, and that also took passengers up to the lifts that were decommissioned in 1924.

King's Cross (L)

The signal box was situated midway along the Northern line's southbound platform. Here one controlled the northbound starting signal and the shunt signal to the loop. The signal box was never manned, save for emergencies, and was mainly used for works trains and stock transfers to and from Acton works. (See photo under Euston). When all Euston control eventually went to Leicester Square on 15 November 1958, so too did King's Cross, where dual control was possible with Covent Garden signal box, which, being closed at night, switched control to Leicester Square prior to closing. Mind you, it was possible to take it any time in an emergency if Covent Garden was in manual operation at King's Cross; the signals bobbed to danger for a fraction as control was taken. When controls were finally transferred to Cobourg Street in November 1969, it didn't happen before the northbound line got diverted in readiness for the Victoria line cross-platform interchange at Euston. The northbound route gained a brand-new platform after making use of the old sidings path. The island platform now became self-contained as the southbound platform. This also gave more control over stock transfers and works trains.

Angel (K)

The only main-line full-sized lever frame on the whole line was installed by the C&SLR. A one-time scissors crossover and a siding similar in layout to Euston, this became the site where trainee inspectors and station foremen were brought to pull the power section switches in the siding. They did so in the company of a divisional inspector and a relief signalman, the latter offering some protection via the box during normal traffic. Always in automatic operation, it was still operational signal-wise, as was the siding back in the mid-fifties, the crossover having been long removed. Interestingly, this siding in the early C&SLR days was the longest on the line, at 858 feet. There was always a problem finding a relief signalman for such an exercise. Eventually I was the only one available for this operation and I wasn't qualified. Not to be put off, I was roped in and I had a five-minute self-instruction on its operation. To release the locks on the levers, one had to operate a large brass plunger secured above each signal, and I had a great time passing trains once the King Lever had been taken out of auto working. I can't recall ever signing a qualification certificate for Angel – it was certainly an education. In 1992, the island platform was converted into a single-line platform similar to Euston, and a new platform route was built, using the old siding as part of the new route for the northbound traffic. The signal box was removed in 1959. There is no record that the lever frame was ever preserved.

Moorgate (M)

Here the original lever frame still contains the Westinghouse Signal & Brake Co. brass plate. Tucked away at the north end of the northbound platform, the signal box was mostly in automatic work. Manned over two shifts, the early shift involved commencing work at Clapham Common signal box from 7.30 am until 10 am; then the signalman went onto Kennington, where he gave the two signalmen their meal breaks, then it was back to Moorgate to finish his shift. The stock transfers from Golders Green to Acton were reversed here and sent back to King's Cross, where they reversed back via the loop up onto the Piccadilly line, before crossing over to the westbound line and on to Acton works. Other than that it was just another emergency crossing point. These small signal boxes were the training grounds for a great many future supervisors.

Moorgate signal box, 1959. Just a south to north crossover, manned over two day shifts. Closed on Sunday, when the late-shift signalman served a shift at Kennington.

London Bridge (P)

This was an unmanned signal box, used solely for emergency crossings. It was normally in automatic operation. A single crossover south of the station provided the only means of reversing in either direction.

Kennington (A in 1890, B in 1924)

My first signal box as a box boy in 1946, this was basically a happy signal box. Two men on each day shift and one on night shift was the total complement. Here the signalmen worked directly from the timetable, as they also did at Camden Town. Each man used lead pointers; should a partner thump the wooden frame, it would cause the other's pointers to jump, which would immediately put the other off sheet, since his pointers would jump out of place. Three descriptions were displayed in a square enunciator set on the frame before each signalman, two for the southern routes and one for the northbound routes. In practice, with the passage of each train, the signalman would press a plunger and one description would step off. It was never automatic then.

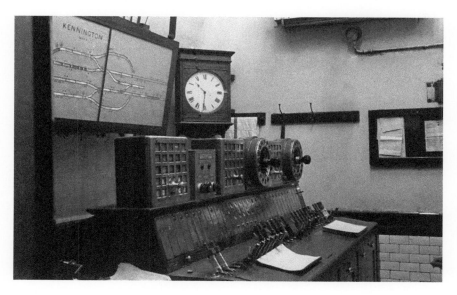

Kennington signal box, 1947.

Kennington lever frame, 1955.

Kennington signal box and relief signalman Bill Deamer, 1955. He was to become one of the automation pioneers within three years.

Kennington and relief signalman George Hughes, 1955.

Kennington interlocking machine room, built in 1957. When the main lever control failed, I had to operate this with instructions regarding train movements via a phone link to the signal box. Having to add an interlocking lever to all your actions was quite an experience. The control fault was corrected after thirty minutes.

Kennington northbound Charing Cross line, platform 1, 1956. The signal box was behind the photographer.

Kennington northbound City line, platform 2, 1956. During the morning rush hour, a great many passengers interchanged here in order to catch an empty train from the loop.

This is how each signalman was able to confirm his timetable findings. Unfortunately the City line was almost all Morden trains, save for the odd Kennington Siding service in the morning rush hour, plus Tooting or Morden depot trains. Consequently there was no way he could keep up without at some time ringing Camden Town or Euston to discover what the next train was to leave them, before counting back how many trains there should be between the two points and then removing all of them until the set train arrived. He would then start again from there.

It was a very busy signal box all through the day shifts. There was a double siding, which is one train on top of another, all under signal control; and a loop on the Charing Cross side. The loop held three trains under signals; in an emergency it could stable five trains end to end. Up until the late fifties, a staff train used to work from the siding into the southbound city platform, and then on to Morden. In later years it started from Stockwell for a short period.

During the rush hour there were trains on the Charing Cross side that were booked not to stop at Kennington on the northbound road, so as to enable a clear run for the following train from the loop that would stop. This non-stop to Waterloo, as it was called, came in handy in later years, enabling a train to pick up three minutes' running time; it was eventually stopped due to the excessive speeds trains used when passing through Kennington empty.

Passing on timetable variations to the next signal box was a standard practice when manual signal boxes controlled the whole line. This occurred at Kennington in particular, when the service was so disorganised. A member of staff would pass on to the local signalman the number of each train (as per the set timetable) when arriving southbound, so that it was routed correctly. During such disruption of the service, it would mean working from a list of train numbers, which contained information forwarded from other signal boxes. It was during these too-frequent times that a northbound Charing Cross train would get routed wrongly into the City platform. Instructing the crew to detrain its passengers and reverse back via the siding, all under signal control, the signalman returned to the signal box and reset the route. In went the train and the correct route was set. I had such an experience and I was surprised when the train came out so quickly and even more surprised to find he had taken his passengers in with him.

If you were able to study a section of timetable relating to the passage of each train, although trains were split into two columns in a timetable, you will soon realise how complex sight and manual action was at Kennington. Were it not for the happy-go-lucky signalman company, it would have been a real hellhole.

Having come directly through the city route missed two signal boxes on the Charing Cross route. They are:

Mornington Crescent (D in 1924, now E)

Having come directly through the city route, I missed two signal boxes on the Charing Cross line. Mornington Crescent was another unmanned signal box. If one required it manned, it would have been difficult, since the only one qualified on site was the lift operator, who also operated the pedestal ticket office, which was contained in the lift. Life was made easier when control was given to Camden Town in 1955, where the single crossover saw a fair amount of use. It became handy when Euston siding was full to be able to reverse stock and, on two occasions, trains were reversed north to south when Camden Town had a serious point failure, and again when a train failed in the Barnet line platform. All eventually transferred to Leicester Square control room, together with Camden Town in 1958.

Strand (C)

This was another emergency crossover point, and it was also the site of the Thames flood gates at the southern end of the station, so the crossover was set north of the station as required. I have known trains to be reversed south to north, sometimes due to very late running, and once when Kennington shut down. The station was closed for a few months in 1977 when the lifts were taken out and escalators installed. The lower platforms were completely refurbished and when re-opened were re-named Charing Cross. On 20 October 1961 its control came under Leicester Square Control Room.

Continuing south from Kennington, the next signal box is

Stockwell (U)

The old southern end C&SLR terminus, now in twin tunnels, the signal box entailed entering a door in one of the cross passages in order to get to the signal cabin, which was situated in the tunnel wall just north of the station. It was very noisy and very dirty and very hot, and I used to wonder how previous tenants stuck it out for an eight-hour shift. It was unmanned from 1926. Most of these small signal boxes were manned around the clock during the Second World War. The siding was north of the station on the southbound side where, as already mentioned, a staff train from Morden stabled for the night for a very short period. This siding no longer exists. Walking around the tunnels one night, I was surprised to find the old tunnel that was used to get the 1890 stock to the surface for maintenance, which now houses a machine room. It is reputed that there is a ghost around Stockwell station. I never saw it but, strangely enough, my bottle of milk used to go bad very quickly overnight. During tunnelling for the Victoria line, just north of Stockwell where the new line passed under the Northern line, the Northern line tunnels sank, and the service was terminated for about two weeks while work was carried out to repair the damage. A special service operated between Clapham Common and Morden while repairs were carried out.

Clapham Common (V)

This was basically the exact reverse of Euston without the siding. The signal box was across the tracks at the north end of the station. Its island platforms put one's heart in one's mouth, since the platforms became so packed during the morning rush hour. I've made use of the scissors crossover many times when Morden or Tooting Broadway was in trouble, reversing those trains stabling further north in order to ease out the congestion. I always recall the northbound starting signal had a very fast-rising train stop and, since the platform was a dead fit for seven cars, a train would start and immediately get tripped, so one spent a great deal of time resetting trips on trains. Control was transferred to Leicester Square on 22 July 1961.

Tooting Broadway (W)

With just a single siding south of the station, this was a very busy signal box during the rush hour. A number of trains were booked to reverse

Tooting Broadway station foreman, Jim Humphries, 1955.

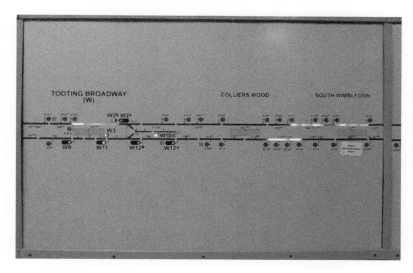

Cobourg station Tooting Broadway diagram, 2012. (Tony Cook)

here to ease the working at Morden, and a reversing service also operated during the off-peak periods. Because of drivers and duty changes for safety reasons, sidings had amber lights fitted in all tunnel sidings at 30-foot intervals to warn drivers where they were.

Another added safety device was a circuit breaker. Should a train attempt to start up without the route being set, the breaker would trip out, removing all current from the siding. The signal box was sited at the south end of the northbound platform down a short slope, so it was actually in the tunnel.

Morden (Y)

Hated by many relief signalmen, due to the signalmen here insisting on a 6.00 am relief time with no trains arriving until 6.29 am. This was a very fast signal box at any time. It was also the site of one of the main and largest depots on the line. One had to be on one's toes during the rush hour here. In the mid-fifties there was hardly a seat available as trains departed north, and one wondered how other users managed to get aboard along the line. Time passed very quickly here since there was always something going on. On my first day of training here, I was told, 'Always use the line of least resistance when bringing trains to and from the depot'. With just three platforms, bringing a train from depot into platforms Nos 1 or 2 prevented any train from entering from the south, so No. 3 platform became the line of least resistance. When stabling trains, No. 1 became the main platform to depot. Basically one used his judgement. Because of the frequency of trains entering service, it wasn't always possible, but then if there were no trains entering on the south, then all platforms were used for trains from the depot.

During the 1955 timetable, when ninety trains operated the service, you will see from the track diagram that there were two routes to depot. The shunter would operate a permission lever on his ground frame to indicate which road he wanted a depot train sent into. Frequently after a route had been cleared he would change his mind, placing the signal to danger and tripping the train. The winter would be the worst time. Trains entering service would become iced up and, although reaching the station, they would have frequent door failures. Here one would instruct the train crew to run empty in order to allow the doors to thaw out in the warm tunnels. In later years, when the train crews became more militant, they would

Morden depot entering service, 1956.

refuse to do this, stating it was an unsafe train even though they were not carrying passengers. Being in close contact with train crews gave one the opportunity to see which trains would turn round quickly and which ones would not. It was times like this, such as helping crews at Colindale make their tea, that paid off in return when emergencies arose.

There were certain practices that took place at certain sections that we thought would be scrapped. For instance, a train requiring assistance would be coupled to the following train and, once empty of passengers, would propel the faulty train, as I had previously explained. In this case it was north up the Barnet branch to a point down the Mill Hill line before reaching the station and being driven back to Highgate depot. In the manual days it would have stopped just north of the furthest crossover at East Finchley and driven back to the depot. Health and safety was practised under automation, where the set route would have to be secured, requiring staff in the tunnels to add clips to points, before having to remove them after the passing of the train. Some of these movements didn't pass without incident. Remember two 'A's' or two 'D's' do not couple.

Another safety operation was applied at Golders Green for trains routed directly across into depot from the northbound direction. If you resided in London in the 1940s or 1950s, you would be aware of the bad fogs. At Golders Green there was an instruction that ran, 'During fog and falling snow, to the cabin you must go'. It wasn't written as such as an instruction. We all thought it was a good way to remind ourselves of this fact. This meant trains had to come into the station and reverse back via the shunt neck, before going to the depot proper, usually placing a spare driver at the other end, thus making the operation a lot faster carrying this out. It was not possible to add a similar command to a programme machine when automation came onto the scene later. This operation had always to be carried out manually.

A similar operation was applied to change overs. This involved taking out a faulty train and replacing it with another fresh service train. Golders Green and Morden were the only places this could be carried out, and all manually. I almost forgot to mention the extra train key when Golders Green was transferred to Cobourg Street in March 1971. It was a means of allowing to pass under first, come instruction without the programme machine stepping on a mark. It was used for an additional train not listed on the programme machine roll. Under automation, one was able to list number-wise any service train that was cancelled, thus allowing the machines on its route to step forward and remove it from the service. Golders Green was one of my favourite signal boxes. It was here you could get out of anything, providing it was carried out safely. Keep all these movements in mind.

As a relief signalman one had to know all the traction current sections throughout the whole line – no mean task, but necessary. In all, there are twenty-seven sections in one direction, which doubling brings the number of sections to fifty-four. Before tunnel sections are switched on, a 'line clear' certificate has to be produced at the sub-station by the section ganger. The failure to do so means the section has to be walked before current is applied to it. Knowing the section is one thing – knowing which sidings are fed from which route is another. Golders Green and Finchley Central are two sites where the feeds become complicated. All depots are alive all day.

Chapter Three

Leicester Square Regulating Room

After a brief spell in operating from a temporary position in a cross-passageway at Kennington, it was eventually re-sited in a temporary control room at Leicester Square in January 1958 – it was a disused lift shaft that was once a Second World War control room. This circular room of 23 feet in diameter was to be our control room for the next eleven or so years. Kennington was to be the first signal box on the Northern line to get programme machines when control was transferred to Leicester Square. Other than the information we had received via printed instructions, no

Leicester Square regulating room, Kennington, January 1959. This was to become a sad state of operation for the next eleven years. Kennington was the first section to be moved here, controlled by one man.

Leicester Square regulating room, Kennington push buttons, 1959. Placed up high, with no training we learnt as we went – mostly on our feet.

Leicester Square regulating room. Kennington control button close-up, 1958.

Leicester Square regulating room with relief signalman Freddy Hobbs and an apprentice. Two-thirds of the working space is taken up by a large steel table, which made control difficult as more sections were added.

Leicester Square temporary regulating room (for eleven years), with relief signalman Peter Mooney attending the new Kennington controls. The four lower windows contained a programme machine for each line's route.

Leicester Square regulating room signal engineers installing Camden Town. Taking a break May 1958. I took the photograph as cover relief signalman that day.

Leicester Square regulating room. Operating Kennington and Camden Town were relief signalmen Bill Deamer and Len Neeves, 1959.

Leicester Square regulating room relief signalman, Phil Langridge, 1958. All the personnel depicted in here, together with five others, were the real operational pioneers in the early days of automating the Northern line. Only two signalmen from Camden Town were part of this number.

Leicester Square final adjustments signal engineer, 1961. Both Strand (now Charing Cross) and Moorgate had just been added. London Bridge came on the following year.

one had any idea, or even a slight idea, how it was all supposed to operate. Gradually we discovered its failings and tried to overcome them, such as programme machines running away. Basically it was a case of forgetting half of what we already knew and adding what we were about to learn.

There were four programme machines at Kennington, one for each route. The south machines were numbers one and two. If number two was calling for a train from CX to Morden, the city train would wait two minutes before an out-of-turn warning would sound. This would be quickly cancelled out to allow the CX train to proceed as timetabled. If, on the other hand, it was decided to allow the city train to proceed, No. 2 machine would go into store until the CX train eventually passed, and then it would step off both trains, and so on. At the close of each day's service, all the programme machines rewound in readiness for the following day's service. They were only removed at weekends when a changed service came into effect on Saturdays and Sundays. Naturally the then-operators were responsible for the changeover of programmes during the night shift.

Working in such a confined space sounds simple; I can tell you that it wasn't. One would spend the whole shift standing up, operating the programme machine controls that were placed below the machine repeater's window. The push buttons were situated higher above the machines. Those of a shorter reach found it tiring, but not difficult. We had all sorts of teething problems; mainly the machines running away or rewinding without our instructions. Having already pointed out the problems faced when the service was disorganised, it seemed to multiply here, gradually getting more complicated as more signal boxes were added to the system.

For instance, if there were three differing routes controlled by one signal, then it had three buttons marked A, B and C. In the case of Kennington, button 'A' was for the loop, button 'B' was for Morden and Button 'C' was for the siding. All three buttons were numbered the same with the exception of the single letter prefix. It was all new to us, but somehow we managed. Having continually to operate each area manually due to service disruptions was how we learnt which button did what. This was modernisation. Eventually we got it sorted out. It was not a system for the older man who had spent years in the same signal box. His vast seniority gave him a first crack at control under modernisation. Two such men didn't and they were offered other posts. Two did and they both became real experts in no time at all.

Difficulties on the line, such as failures of track circuits, point failures or signal failures, were where you came into your own. It wasn't too stressful, only having to deal with Kennington. As more signal boxes were added, the stress became more consuming. Thanks to the odd spare relief signalman dropping in and helping out, some of the regulars were prevented from ending up in the funny farm. It was both hot and noisy when the service was disruptive. At first, two men were on duty per day shift for Kennington and one on night shift. The second man acted as a spare, while also learning the procedures. Camden Town came in next in June 1958. It too was then moved to the same disused lift shaft in Leicester Square station, where four programme machines were fitted that were to control movements through all four junctions. Another man was appointed. Each was able to give the other a break and there was provision to make tea, which was a godsend on its own, and we drank gallons of the stuff. We now had Kennington and Camden Town in operation at both sides of the central control area. At this time, both were controlled by just two men on each of the day shifts and one on night shift. Fortunately, there was always an extra relief signalman around, mainly to get their feet under the table and learn as much as they could.

This was where the strong team spirit came into being. You felt more at ease knowing there was someone on hand to help you get out of difficulties. It may sound strange to an outsider. It was like having more than one brain. Getting assistance from a colleague, his knowledge was identical to your own and he would do what you were thinking and you got on with your own participation. For instance, there would be one operating buttons, and the other on the phone passing all these changes onto Golders Green, East Finchley to the north or Tooting, not forgetting Euston and Moorgate on the City line. This became time-consuming and far too much for one man to deal with.

Once Camden Town was fitted in, this was where the confusion really began. On the City line, there were still two manned signal boxes, Euston and Moorgate, not to mention other manned signal boxes at both north and south ends of the line. The passing and receiving of information from these areas just added to the confusion during a disruptive service. Manual operation was the only means of obtaining some sort of rhythm in the service during this time; it became more frequent as more signal boxes were transferred.

At first, when Archway was added to Leicester Square's control, another man was added, one of the two previous signalmen from Camden Town. Then Euston was added in November 1958; the Strand and Moorgate were added in 1961. This was all to be repeated when control was moved to Cobourg Street later. The ex-Camden Town signalmen were the only two without full line training. The remainder of the operators were all relief signalmen like myself. Since we were all known to each other, a powerful team was to form that would grow and last for a great many years.

Having already noted and experienced the complications involved with many of the larger signal boxes, I have already mentioned that the mind boggled as to what effect automating the whole line would have, and how it would affect the service, should a failure on the line happen – and it did, far too regularly for our liking. The big question was, how would a minimum of operating staff cope in such an event?

Modernisation really did arrive with a vengeance in the late 1950s and early 1960s, together with total confusion as one by one – and I mean one by one – signal boxes in the central area, both Charing Cross and City lines, were eventually closed and their control added to that at Leicester Square control room. We had to learn this new operation as we went – I have already explained that we received no training. As ex-relief signalmen, we were all aware of the manual side, whereas later newcomers were not. It all came down to our experience of the areas and having to accept that one button now controlled both the signal and the points. We attempted to teach newcomers, who were all ex-signalmen from other lines; they eventually got by with our help. In the meantime, management decided on a new name for the operatives. They were to be titled 'traffic regulators', carrying the same grade status as station masters.

Again I should mention the heat given off by the lamps in the diagram in such a restricted space was tremendous, and this was only changed where trains were, being in a section that was red instead of the black that we were used to. When Morden and Tooting Broadway were automated, their control was placed in an office at street level, next to the whole Underground railway systems line controller's room in 1962, which overlooked Charing Cross road. Again, the passing of information was the greatest downfall when the service was disrupted. When working in the old signal-boxes era, one was able to view passing trains, thus being in a position to correct missed information errors. (Each train had a number displayed on the front cab.) Under this new scheme, you were totally blind. No more hydraulic sounds of points being operated. All movements were now done in complete silence. You pressed a button and hoped it worked.

I should also mention A4-size notices in light-yellow covered booklet form were issued to all members of the staff, which described changes in these areas in what we called 'The Yellow Peril'. Signal engineers learnt our movements from the still-maintained mechanical interlocking now housed in separate buildings at the original sites. In many cases, the original signal boxes became the home of these hydraulically operated interlocking machines. Sites such as Edgware, Golders Green, High Barnet, Finchley Central, East Finchley and Morden eventually all had their own operational peculiarities, which I have already explained. Having all this personal operational knowledge was to see this operation eventually work.

During the period from 1969 to 1978, new types of signals were gradually being introduced throughout the line. We called them 'creepers'. Basically a train had to almost come to a stop at these signals before they eventually cleared. Installed to stop the spate of trains over-shooting stop signals that protected points or junctions, they became a real bind until crews got used to them. The standard of training for crews was still high; the standard of learning was not.

Euston, which operated a rush-hour terminating service, and the Piccadilly line link at King's Cross were now almost the last additions. All this was controlled by four men (including the Morden part), plus any spare relief signalmen who were available, since we had less work to do now. East Finchley came on to Leicester Square control room on 24 June 1961.

I will attempt to explain a few of the technicalities involved with the trouble-free operations of the Leicester Square situation. Each train was dispatched with a destination that was coded from the first four letters of the alphabet. This coding had always existed and was so simple to understand. For instance, any description containing a D was always routed via Charing Cross. All codes without D were routed via the City route. It worked in both directions. There was just a number of small variations relating to a train's final destination. For instance, Edgware via Charing Cross was CD. Barnet was ABCD and Mill Hill ABD. Golders

Green was AD and Colindale was BD. Euston via the City northbound code was just D. This was the only deviation from the same codes used for the city route. There were variations such as train testing between Golders Green depot to Edgware and the return to Golders Green depot. These movements were only carried out after the peak service had ended. You can check them all on the PTI code chart later.

Here I have to mention Kennington siding that was signalled for two seven-car trains. For a train that is stabled this far down, the crew would enter a passage at the end of the siding that would take them onto the Oval northbound station platform – then it would be a train back to Kennington. This practice was stopped after an incident. Now just a single train has use of it during service periods. You would advise staff at Oval to inform a set train to make a stop at Kennington siding to collect the stabled train's crew.

By far the greatest curse was out-of-turn working. Imagine a train from Barnet leaving the loop, now on the path of an Edgware train due to return to Colindale. The train for Barnet would pick up the destination for the Edgware train without anyone noticing. When the train reached Camden Town, the driver would stop and question the route since it was really a Barnet train. This was a continuing problem, which got worse as more signal boxes were added to this control room.

You might have noticed when travelling on the line in the seventies that each train had a letter placed at each end. This only applies to 1938 Tube stock. It was A on the north end and D on the south end. This indicated that only A & D would couple together, as I've already mentioned. In the mid-fifties, after the rush hour both morning and evening, trains were divided into four cars for the Charing Cross service and some three cars for the City service. Those not required were stabled in readiness for the evening rush hour. Barnet for instance did not provide a City service off-peak. In order to make this scheme work, one needed to know at recoupling time which way round Kennington terminating trains were before you dispatched them north. It always had to be 'A' leading north. Were this not so, the train would be reversed via the siding. Even so, some slipped through, which created problems at terminuses north. Morden's problem was receiving too many three-cars and no four-cars with which to couple up, so they had to be shunted temporarily to the depot until required. With only three platforms it was a little scary at times. You have to remember all this took place during the manual operational period. It doesn't bear thinking about, this system still being in practice during automation.

I have explained that each programme roll had the entire service on it for each control section. Should a train's code not agree with the machine, a single-stroke warning bell sounded. The operator would normally operate the first-come-first-served application and the train would go on its way without hindrance. At termination points, programme machines automatically added a train's destination. When the service was disrupted, this had to be completed manually by the operator. Terminating trains at Golders Green, Colindale and Edgware at the same time was a plan for disaster, and there were plenty – not to mention the distractions of telephone calls.

In the meantime, the Victoria line was being constructed and was to be controlled in a new building at Euston in Cobourg Street. It was here in the same room that the Northern line's control centre was eventually to be established. How we all managed to survive working in this hellhole for a little over ten years still amazes me when I think about it. Euston, Tooting Broadway and Moorgate signal boxes would have been a luxury after all this. We began to move in to the new control room from October 1969 that was to become our new spacious home. Gradually each area was connected up until the whole line came on stream.

Chapter Four

Cobourg Street Regulating Room

The room, being circular, was laid out thus – the control desks were arranged in a half circle. The Edgware–Hampstead and Barnet were added in 1971. Archway was already there. Two men shared these two sections, one for each branch. Each area's control buttons were situated in sliding drawers beside each regulator. Next came the Camden Town, Euston, and Mornington Crescent, Moorgate area. Here the operator shared a desk with the Strand, London Bridge, Kennington, Clapham Common and Stockwell operator. On the only single desk were the controls for Tooting Broadway and Morden. Both the latter and the Barnet areas were unmanned at night, this being taken on by the Kennington and Edgware man. All in all, it wasn't such a bad arrangement.

Morden through to the central area was now all linked up. So, for a few weeks, life was a little hairy, in that changes to the service had to be forwarded by phone to Finchley Central and Golders Green, since Golders Green was in control to Edgware, and so forth. This will give you some idea of the chaos when the whole system was all linked. We were all still cursed with having to pass information to each other.

Five men with a midday relief position operated each day shift, with only three operators on night shift, not including the Victoria line's one man. Each regulator was rostered to carry out duties on all control positions, including the Victoria line when it became fully functional. When there was an incident such as a signal or point failure, everyone helped out in their own way. Diverting traffic, it was all hands to help out. This is where such a strong team operated best, since each had the same local knowledge as the other. Our experience at the Leicester Square control room was an asset in one direction, since we were no longer responsible for the changeover of programme machine rolls. The area signal department's resident at these sites carried out this task. Being able to sit down, even when you had to operate buttons, was a luxury. Eventually we got used to making use of the automatic functions such as 'First come, first served' acknowledging changes of destination, plus the cancellation set up and the extra train key. It would be far too complicated to explain why that was required during the rush hour. There was the odd occasion when a train was given a wrong route and, instead of stopping and questioning it, it carried on as though it was on the correct path. Naturally its official path had to be removed from the programme machine and its destination had to be confirmed. Now we had to note which train it was, following it though its new path so as to enable the next man to make sure he operated the extra train key for its real passage and the first-come key. I should point out that a Charing Cross train routed via the City had approximately twelve minutes plus added to its journey. This either had to be adjusted with a possible turn short along the way or we just let it run and hoped some of that time could be regained by a quick turn around at its real termination point.

The mind really boggled, in that you were immediately aware of an area's problems and you prepared yourself for the overflow, as it depended on how you dealt with the problem. A fellow regulator who was less involved would jump in and help. You can't blame programme machines for outside failures or faults. As I keep mentioning, we were a team and, as such, life was a little more pleasant. Interestingly, the line controllers knew us all and we had a pretty free hand when there was a service problem. As long as they were kept informed of the changes, they could deal with the train crew changes required. There were four relief staff to cover holidays and sickness, and there was still Park Junction at Highgate to cover, plus Moorgate and Drayton Park on the Northern & City line.

Gradually, even with staff transferred from other lines, we became a stronger team. The rostering was interesting, in that you would have four members of the team for, say, two weeks, then a new team for five weeks. A single member every week left your team for a different shift. There were always interesting conversations during quieter moments between the operators. Stranger still, many of these work mates I had known since a lad and some during my relief signalman days.

All management staff in those early days were once ex-railway-operating staff themselves until, one by one, they retired and were eventually

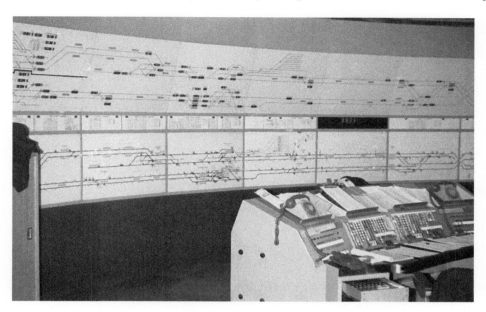

Cobourg Street Barnet and Edgware branch desk, 1970. This was a two-man desk during the day, but just one-man at night.

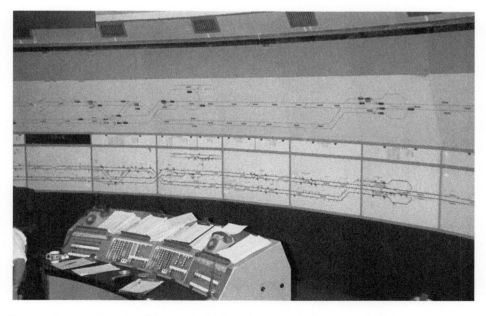

Cobourg Street Camden Town and Kennington desk, 1970. This was a two-man desk over twenty-four hours. The Kennington man took over the Morden desk at night.

Cobourg Street, with the chairman, 1975.

Cobourg Street, Ron Noon and Howard 'Tich' Thomas, 1970.

Cobourg Street, Team Retirement 2: Les Friend, Fred Bayman, Ken Day, Freddy Hobbs, Owen Smithers, George Dyer, Unknown, 1990.

replaced by business-trained people and characters, with no real railway background; temperaments began to clash and tensions start to appear. When long-time companion regulators began to retire or die before their time, semi-trained personnel replaced them. When I left, women came in the forefront much later and many found it too much of a mental strain. Money tends to do that to people.

Here I was, working in a room with men I had known since my early days. Some I trained with and some I had trained. The topics of conversation livened a shift up and created a pleasant atmosphere and a sense of camaraderie one usually only found in the armed services.

Situated behind us was the line controller. The old hands were fine; it was business as usual. As they retired and a younger man took their place, his power became rather unbearable. Gone were the 'do it and tell me afterwards' days; in came the hesitancy and a God-like attitude we had never met before. It soon became evident in the early seventies that it was a case of 'let them get on with it'. Being in a position to see all, it became worry, worry and worry, as far as they were concerned. We did our thing as normal. In fairness, many of the controllers were very good and were prepared to listen, whereas others were not. I guess we were all too laidback in our work and this upset some controllers, who seemed to take a small every-day incident, which we dealt with in our usual way, and blow it out of all proportion.

Although two floors up, there was no outlook, since the windows were at least 20 feet from the ground. Here we were able to sit in a comfortable chair and relax a little, and let the machines do the work. A deputation from Camden Council visited after we had been in operation for a while. One councillor was heard to remark, 'I've seen pigs in better surroundings'. It's a pity they didn't pay a little more attention to some of the conditions to which we had previously been accustomed. No toilets, no running water, and a single half-hour break in an eight-hour shift. Here we were shown off to all and sundry from all over the world. During the dark days of the early seventies, the misery line was headlines. (The daily press gave the title). We had a BBC film crew holding hot lights over us as we tried to work. If it's ever shown again, I'm the guy on the Kennington section.

One service operation that was carried out via programme machine was the Sunday Finchley Central–Mill Hill shuttle. You have already discovered that weekdays, Saturdays and Sundays had their own separate programmes. These would be changed at close of traffic on a Friday night and replaced by the following day's service programmes.

Programme machines were only situated where a reversing point or junction was situated. None of the emergency crossovers had programme machines, since they operated automatically where through traffic was concerned. There were no repeat programme machines in the room at Cobourg Street, just a visual display at each junction displaying the number of the next train at that point. Additional trains were catered for by the operation of the extra-train switch, and the train proceeds according to its description without stepping the programme machine at that point.

There are three main controls over a programme machine area. 'Push-button control' is manual operation. 'First come, first served' means that the first train to reach a certain point gets the route, according to its destination. This was handy when the service was a little disjointed and, of course, programme-machine only. This will only allow trains through a junction that are called for on the programme machine roll. Other modes such as 'programme machine acknowledge', which would change a train's wrong description to a correct one, were a great advantage. To set up a train cancellation, one sets up the number of the train on each machine the train's path is recorded on, and when its number is reached it automatically steps off the machine. This makes it possible to set a cancellation up through the whole of the train's route along the line. ATO that was installed later was to make many of these controls redundant.

Referring back to the very poor Saturday service during the late sixties and seventies, having moved into Cobourg Street, it brought to one's notice the reluctance of line controllers even to attempt to do anything about it. Regulators frequently did things off their own backs, such as extending a Colindale train onto Edgware and short-tripping it at Tooting Broadway in the south in order to regain the lost fifteen minutes of running time. There were many instances where an emergency timetable was introduced due to special works or the shortage of rolling stock and I could never understand why a Saturday was any different from any other day, and that all trains were routed to Mill Hill, Barnet and Edgware in the north and Kennington and Morden in the south. Providing the public knew of the train's destination, they could at least change, say, at Euston for the Victoria line in order to reach the West End. It made one feel quite useless sitting there and watching trains being pulled out of service through lack of staff.

I was attracted to a statement made in London Transport 1940s minute records:

The Northern line remains a vital component of the underground network and carries 800,000 customers daily. (In 1940) It has the most complex network of any tube line, and requires considerable knowledge and skill to manage in the event of significant disruption.

On 31 August 1986, Positive Train Identification (PTI) was introduced, at the beginning only from Morden to Kennington. It means the regulator does not have to set up the train's next destination at termini and that information transmitted forward through each junction also enables the regulator to see exactly where on the line a train is. A new line diagram, containing light-emitting diode (LED) indicators, was to be installed, replacing the existing line diagram. The new diagram would contain

Cobourg Street control room 1, 2014. (Tony Cook)

Cobourg Street control room 2, 2014. (Tony Cook)

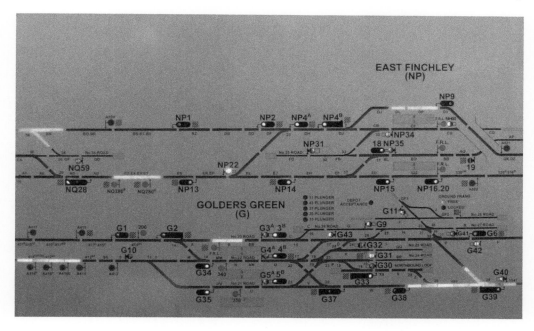

Cobourg Street, East Finchley and Golders Green diagram, 2014. Can you imagine all these signals disappearing under automation? (Tony Cook)

two types of indicator – green for information received from the PTI equipment and yellow for information from other sources. What is termed as an interrogator is secured within the track and interrogates the information the train sends out when it passes over it. They are placed at various points on the line, in particular at junctions or terminating points. This information is transmitted to the computer at Cobourg Street control centre. The information is then used to give a position display to the regulator; it automatically routes the train at junctions, as well as providing information to station platform displays and, in the control room, each train number and destination, whether it is in service or not. If a train has a fault regarding transmitting information, three zeroes relating to the train's number and three crosses indicating the train's destination are displayed on the diagram. Being able to contact the driver via radiophone, the driver is advised to check his set up. Failing to do so will result in the train being held at a signal point leading into a junction until this information is corrected. Should a train's route be changed during its journey, its new destination is displayed on the train but not on station platform displays until it reaches its next interrogator. Station displays would see a 'correction' flashing, indicating that they should check the front of the train when it arrives to see the correct destination displayed. With out-of-turn working, particularly at junctions, i.e. Camden Town and Kennington, the next station display will automatically change in relation to its destination. The Kennington interrogator diagram will give some indication as to how this system operates.

Here the driver sets up his route information via a keypad. The driver, upon opening up the train, enters the train destination (there is a list of the TD codes on the cab wall) and the duty number the train operator is carrying, before connecting the handheld radio to the train. A transmitter is located below the leading car, through which the information he sets up is transmitted forward when the train moves off. There is also a rotary switch that indicates to the regulator if the train is in or out of service (stabled). Drivers of trains set up their destination codes (already shown on the list earlier) on their train so that, when moving off, their destination is transmitted via track aerials and transmitted to platform destination signs and to all programme machines en route.

The exception is: in the case of a train entering service from Morden depot to Edgware via Charing Cross, the train driver must set up 'Edgware via Charing Cross' in the depot. In the case of a train entering service from Golders Green depot to Golders Green station and thence to Morden via the City, the train driver must set-up 'Morden via City' in depot. The later also applies if the route is directly southbound from depot. At the last station, prior to their destination point, the driver sets up his next destination. If it's to be routed to depot then he does nothing. If a train is diverted, or cancelled, the system then updates the appropriate machines along the line; thus there is no need to input cancellations or activate extra train keys on every machine. As long as the system is up to date, it keeps all the machines up to date. This was to be a vast improvement to what we had to deal with in those early Leicester Square and Cobourg Street operations.

If the equipment detects a train on the line not equipped for PTI, or a train with defective equipment or a non-recognizable code, the following will be displayed on the regulator's line diagram:

'xxx' – train destination/description
ooo – train number

The regulator must arrange for the train driver to be contacted to ensure that the PTI equipment is working and the correct codes are inputted into the equipment. If all trains are shown as above, the Signal Report centre must be informed immediately.

This added function had its problems, since it seemed many drivers didn't know how to set it all up in their cabs. When the 1995 rolling stock trains were introduced, this procedure was made simpler and just one man controlled all trains. Early in 2008, a point was brought to light regarding the diversity of the Northern line and its junctions at Camden Town and Kennington, one relating to its service patterns. It was proposed that trains can start from Morden in the south and go to Edgware, High Barnet or Mill Hill East via either Charing Cross or the Bank, just as they've always done. While this pattern is most welcome for the passengers, it represents a big problem for the operators. If anything goes wrong, the service continuity quickly falls apart over the whole line. Even when it's running smoothly, having to work the various services through the junctions at Kennington and Camden Town, both at either end of the two central area branches, limits the service of trains to twenty per hour on each branch. Once the new signalling was installed in 2014, this was expected to get up to twenty-four trains an hour. In its previous form, it could never reach the thirty trains possible on other upgraded routes. The ideal solution was splitting the line into two parts, one covering Kennington and Edgware via Charing Cross, the other Morden to High Barnet and Mill Hill East via Bank. This would require changing trains for a very large number of passengers at Kennington and Camden Town or Euston, raising health and safety concerns. Camden Town is particularly vulnerable in this respect, with its tortuous and complicated connecting passages between the two routes. Forced changes there would mean up to 400 or more passengers changing from each arriving train to the next, and having to clash with passengers passing in the opposite direction. This was put into practise in 2002 as a trial, I understand.

In 2002, train operator step-ups were introduced at Morden during the peak service in order to increase the turn-round frequency of trains. It meant a train operator would give his train up to another operator and he himself would take on another in a similar fashion. This gave the northbound route a three-minute continuous service.

At 10.01 am on Sunday 19 October 2003, northbound Northern line train 11 (the 09.19 Morden–High Barnet via Bank) became derailed as it entered platform number 3 at Camden Town. The rear of the train sustained considerable damage, with the sixth (and last) car becoming detached from the fifth and coming into contact with the tunnel wall where the line splits to go to Edgware (left) and Barnet (right). Services were suspended between Hampstead–East Finchley and Charing Cross–Euston (City), with special bus services introduced as a part replacement. The Charing Cross branch service was reinstated (Edgware–Morden) at 06.30 on Wednesday 29 October, and East Finchley–Euston at about 11.30 am on Thursday 30 October. However, from that date, services were arranged to operate via Charing Cross (Barnet and Mill Hill) or via Bank (Edgware), with the northbound point work at Camden Town junction being secured for through running.

In 2004 the timetable reverted back to the old system, with Edgware via CX and the City south. It was the same from the Barnet branch. There was to be no short timetabled reversing anywhere on the whole line. The Northern line was to see many timetable changes from here on, in order to appease the travelling public. There was an off-peak shuttle service from Mill Hill to Finchley Central, to and from platform 1. In order to make a connection south, one had to traverse a footbridge over the tracks; I am not sure how the disabled dealt with this. A plan was put forward to extend this service to East Finchley, thus making the cross-platform interchange easier. The train would then have to shunt via the siding and back into the northbound platform for its next trip. Somehow I don't think this will happen, unless an additional train is added to this service.

The peak services were extensively re-cast in 2008, with sole thought to increasing a maximum service during the busiest hour in each of the morning peaks. The northbound services during this period segregated, so that all Charing Cross trains operate to the Edgware branch and all City trains operate to High Barnet and Mill Hill East. Therefore, there is no train northbound from Kennington to High Barnet via Charing Cross after 06.33 until 10.08. Similarly, there is no train northbound from Kennington to Edgware via Bank after 06.28 until 10.03, apart from two isolated journeys at 08.36 and 09.02.

Now you can see how so many previously manual tasks were removed through the advances of modern technology. No more having a member of the local staff sited on the southbound CX platform at Kennington, passing on the train number of each train as it arrives in order to apply the correct route to said trains when the service became too disorganised.

Interestingly, the now-approved extension from Kennington to Battersea will include an additional station at Nine Elms. The line would be connected to the reversing loop south of Kennington station, so that all the Battersea trains would come from the Charing Cross route. The problem with this new terminus at Battersea is that it would have the capacity to eventually reverse a thirty-train-per-hour service. This is something the Underground planners will be possibly looking into.

Automatic Train Operation (ATO) was eventually introduced on the Northern line in 2013, but only on the East Finchley–Barnet section of the line – at least until the resignalling programme progresses. It commenced with a 'training section' between Highgate and High Barnet, which will be used at weekends to instruct drivers in how to drive under the protection of the new system. They'll need this to develop new driving skills in using the cab displays instead of observing lineside signals. I believe this process is the Seltrac40 Transmissions-Based Train Control (TBTC) system provided by Thales.

In the meantime full signalling conversion will work north from Morden in stages, with the first section covering the line to Clapham North. Important lessons had been learnt during the building of the Jubilee line and so, at the same time, the first part of the new Highgate control centre will be commissioned for this area only, with the old Cobourg Street-based control desks for the old signalling having been de-commissioned. During this upgrade, the new Highgate controllers will see the unconverted bits of the line using Tracker Net, London Underground's real-time train-location monitoring system. TBTC is a transmission-based system via inductive loops installed between the running rails. It is effectively a moving-block system, since there are no block joints or overlaps. Trains report their current position every second and are given a target destination point every three seconds, ensuring a safe separation distance. Train performance can increase with higher top speeds. This is an Automatic Train Operation (ATO) system. ATO was finally introduced over the whole of the Northern line in 2014. It is similar to that in use on the Victoria line, with a great many modifications. Plans have been bandied around for some time as to the possibility that Unmanned Train Operation (UTO) could be introduced on the Underground in the future. Although non-passenger-carrying, the Post Office railway in London had operated as such since 1937.

The Victoria line experienced UTO quite unexpectedly. A driver closed the doors of his train and pressed the proceed button. The train didn't start. Looking back, he saw a door light on and left his train to close the door physically. To his amazement, when the door finally closed, he watched his train depart driverless to the next station. It meant drastic circuitry alterations to prevent this happening again. There is a strong possibility that UTO could eventually be introduced in the future. This improvement would take automatic operations really into the twenty-first century. It's interesting to note that, in July 2013, the mayor of London, Boris Johnson, said he will never again buy a train with a driver's cab and that the Underground will be fully automated by the 2020s.

Just out of interest: after the Victoria line control was moved to Northumberland Park depot, the original desk and diagram were completely saved and now reside in a railway carriage at The Electric Railway Museum in Coventry, where they hope to recreate a working simulation of its actual operation.

New innovations, such as doing away with programme-machine rolls and replacing them with electronic miniature programme pods as small as a mobile phone, with the whole service now on a memory stick, are really taking us into the fast-growing electronic age, which will eventually reveal even more advancement in railway control in the future.

In 2014 Cobourg Street closed officially. All controls were transferred to Highgate in a new building at the rear of Highgate depot. The only problem I can see here is getting there for a 6.00 am start, depending on where one resides. In a gathering for the final official closure of Cobourg Street on 24 April 2015, Mr Pat Hansberry, operations director for JN, said,

Our upgrade on the Northern line has been a fantastic success – but a shiny new control room (at Highgate) is no good unless it has people with the knowledge to get the best from it. Many of our current Service Control team either worked alongside you, or were directly trained by you. The systems may have come a long way, but the principles are the same, and we'd never have got to where we are today without that cascade of knowledge. On behalf of the millions of customers and hundreds of staff who have benefitted from your expertise in operating the Northern and Victoria lines over the years – thank you.

A great pity so many of us have passed on. It would have been nice to know that you were appreciated back in the sixties and seventies. The Cobourg Street centre was first opened in 1968 and was to become home to generations of both Northern and Victoria line regulators. It signalled four different stocks of Northern line trains alone, as well as the introduction of remote points-securing equipment, direct signallers' telephones to drivers and a whole host of other milestones in the refinement of service control across LU. The final train movement was made from Cobourg Street in 2014. Highgate and Northumberland Park are now the control centres for both the Northern and Victoria lines respectively.

Chapter Five

Highgate Control Centre

I have already mentioned the Programme Train Indicator codes, which the drivers would input and set up in their cabs. The train would then transmit this information, via the onboard transponders, and this would be picked up via the PTI aerials on the track. The code would then be translated into the appropriate describer code to platform destination displays and the train's route to signals. Then there is the VOBC (Vehicle On-Board Computer), which receives the commands directly from the Vehicle Control computer at Highgate control room, which effectively drives and signals when a train is in automatic mode. This bears repeating, as it's important that you keep all this in mind.

Since all trains are fully visible on the control-room diagrams, a regulator could still change the platform describers as well. For instance, if a Morden train approaching Tooting Broadway south in an emergency had to be reversed at Tooting Broadway, one could switch on the southbound platform describer on the desk. It would display a Morden train destination in the button. One could then select a Tooting description, then put the site into 'First come, first served' operation and the route will automatically clear for the siding. A flashing indication on the driver's display panel informs him of this change of route. Once in the siding, all the related programme machines know where the train is and, at the appointed northbound path, the train will be routed as normal.

The new electronic programme machines operate in exactly the same way as the old ones. The original Melinex-roll housing was completely removed in the 1990s, and the new electronic gizmo was slotted in to take its place. All the connections were and are the same as before. The timetable is now stored on a USB key, and they can still be stepped manually at any site remotely. As long as the train list is kept up to date,

Highgate depot sidings, 1958.

Highgate depot, south-end tracks removed, 1985. (Brian Hardy)

Highgate control training room, 2015.

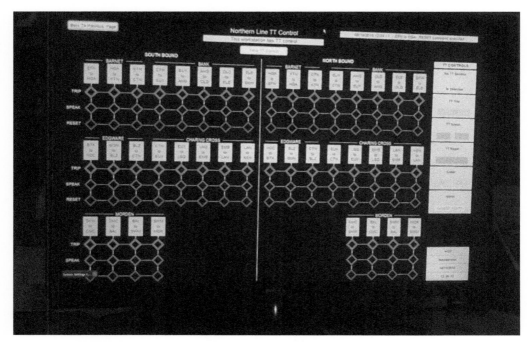

Highgate control training room, train data simulation, 2015.

Highgate control room programme machine, data section, 2015.

Highgate control room regulator's position, one of four.

Highgate control room – the same desk from a different angle in order to capture all the screens. The two upper screens show the whole line as a repeater of those shown below. All screens show the identical information.

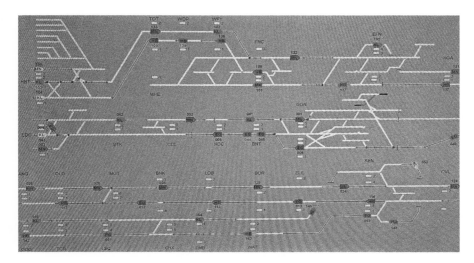

Highgate control room, Barnet–Golders Green–Kennington display, 2015.

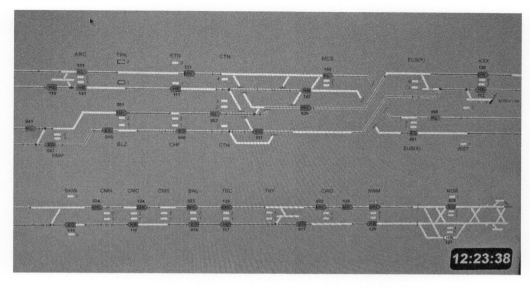

Highgate control room, Camden Town–Morden display, 2015.

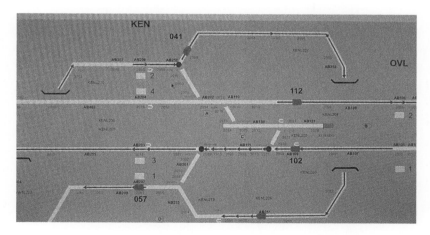

Highgate control room, Kennington display. Here you can clearly see each train and its number, plus the freedom of route, in this enlarged section, 2015.

you can follow the train along the whole system. As previously mentioned, if a train is diverted or cancelled, the system then updates the appropriate machines along the line, and thus there is no need to input cancellations or extra trains on every machine, as it's done automatically. So long as the system is up to date, it will keep all the machines up to date. This system had already been installed at Cobourg Street in 2012 and is now transferred here to Highgate.

A personal visit to the control room in October 2015 was a real eye-opener. With no disrespect, it was like entering a large video-games room. These new line diagrams were amazing. Everything you wanted to see was there in front of you. Being able to enlarge any section on the diagram was an eye opener to me. The silence in the room was amazing. Talking with some of the operators, we were able to exchange experiences of Cobourg Street. It was sad knowing all those earlier regulators never got to see this final development. All the operations outside were now completely automatic. It was during my visit that I discovered there were eight VCCA (Vehicle Control Centre Areas) covering the whole line. The only human connection is the driver of a train opening and closing the doors at stations. I was amazed to learn there were no longer any signals that I grew up with anywhere on the whole of the Northern line. I should add that trains to Highgate depot now operate a plunger at the south end of East Finchley platform. Once set, the train proceeds to depot. The same function is used to gain access to the depot siding only for works trains. Safety factors that just amazed me are everywhere. I'm glad that it has been my good fortune to have lived long enough to actually see the end result of all the misery and brain shattering we all went through, so as to achieve this amazing operation.

Training

In all, 551 train operators had to be trained for the Northern line, two weeks per person. Seven service managers and thirty-two service controllers will train for six weeks per person (assuming they are already multi-skilled). 458 customer service assistants are to receive a briefing. 271 station supervisors need two days' training. This amounts to 1,319 staff in total, plus duty managers, operating officials, etc. The cab simulators have been replaced, two at Edgware and one at Morden.

Life really is stranger than fiction. During the days of the 'misery line' tag, one would read in the local press letters of protest at the overcrowding and having to travel like animals. This always brought a smile to our faces. If they knew how many trains were taken out of service containing vomit, infestations and the like, it made us believe we were transporting animals.

The amount of variety was amazing. There was always something going on that would enliven the shift. We all learnt, as I have previously mentioned, the new Victoria line when it came into being in all its four stages. All in all, they were happy times, since everyone knew everyone, including outside staff, so it was a nice family atmosphere, only changing when new staff took vacant posts as those long-serving staff moved on or reached retirement age.

Times change and progress advances towards computerised regulating rooms. This was a project started in 1955 that plodded on in its various stages into 2014. I'll always recall the words of an old signalman at Camden Town who said, 'They will never automate Camden Town – it's too complicated'. He just lived long enough to see it happen.

In the meantime, I reluctantly resigned in November 1978 for personal domestic reasons. My interest and friends I left behind kept me in touch with the changes that later took place, which kept my passionate interest flowing. I trust this expanded reference on both the history and the switch-over from manual operation to automatic operation has been informative as well as instructional. Making use of my retentive memory for me has meant reliving those exciting moments all over again.

I recently heard that many of my old workmates sadly have now passed on. This book is written for and dedicated to them.

Acknowledgements

The author and publisher would like to thank the following people/ organizations for permission to use copyright material in this book:

The Railway Gazette's 'Improving London's Transport' publication, 1946;
Tony Cook and Brian Hardy for giving permission to use their photographs;
The use of speeches and official notes from LU staff;
All remaining photographs are the property of the author.

I would like to dedicate this work to all the original pioneers, who with just their basic outside knowledge took on this task with their usual enthusiasm. They were:

William Boyce	(Leicester Sq. & Cobourg Street)
Dudley Barker-Hemming	(Leicester Sq. & Cobourg Street)
Freddy Hobbs	(Leicester Sq. & Cobourg Street)
Leonard Neeves	(Leicester Sq. & Cobourg Street)
Peter Mooney	(Leicester Sq. & Cobourg Street)
Alfred Prouse	(Leicester Sq. & Cobourg Street)
Leslie Heartfield	(Leicester Sq. & Cobourg Street)
Owen Smithers	(Leicester Sq. & Cobourg Street)
Sidney Broom	(Leicester Sq.)
George Dyer	(Leicester Sq. & Cobourg Street)
Mitchel-Gears	(Leicester Sq. & Cobourg Street)
William 'Bill' Deamer	(Leicester Sq. & Cobourg Street)
Leslie Friend	(Leicester Sq. & Cobourg Street)

Phillip Langridge	(Leicester Sq. & Cobourg Street)
Arthur Langridge	(Leicester Sq. & Cobourg Street)
Howard 'Tich' Thomas	(Cobourg Street)
Colin Jermy	(Cobourg Street)
Ronald Noon	(Cobourg Street)
Robert Noon	(Cobourg Street)
Gordon Cayless	(Cobourg Street)
Keneth Day	(Cobourg Street)
Jim Officer	(Cobourg Street)
Raymond Rigsby	(Cobourg Street)
Roy Toppin	(Cobourg Street)
Ted Darvill	(Cobourg Street)
Sidney Cox	(Cobourg Street)
George McCullum	(Cobourg Street)
Sam Ward	(Cobourg Street)
Alan Hore	(Cobourg Street)
John Wilkinson	(Cobourg Street)
Richard Tate	(Cobourg Street)

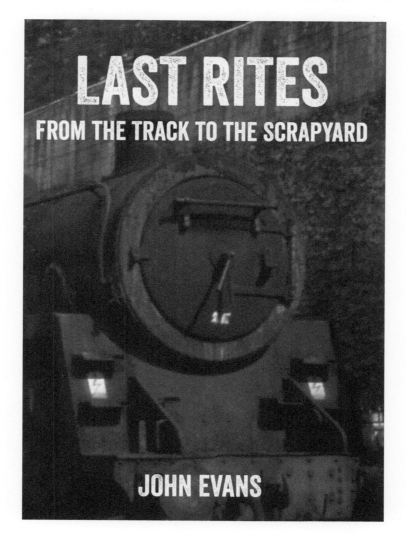

Last Rites

John Evans

John Evans takes a fond look back at steam engines scrapped in the
1960s.

978 1 4456 5498 0
128 pages, illustrated throughout

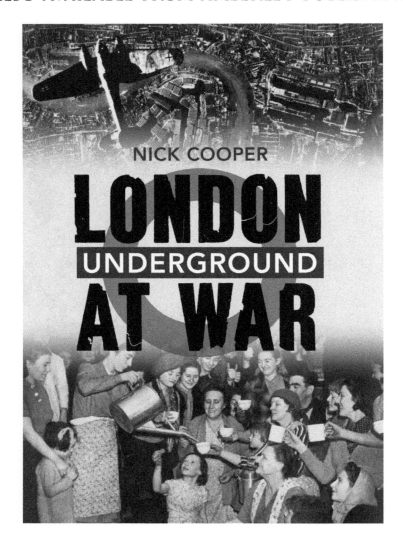

London Underground at War

Nick Cooper

Nick Cooper explores the impact of the war on the running of the
Underground and the role it played in so many people's lives.

978 1 4456 2201 9
160pages, illustrated throughout

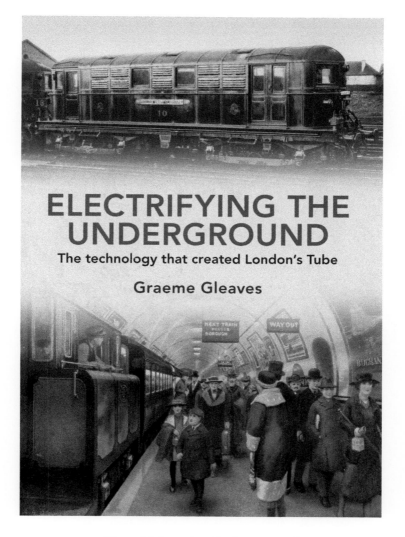

Electrifying the Underground

Graeme Gleaves

The arrival of electric traction transformed London's fledging
Underground system.

978 1 4456 2203 3
128 pages, illustrated throughout

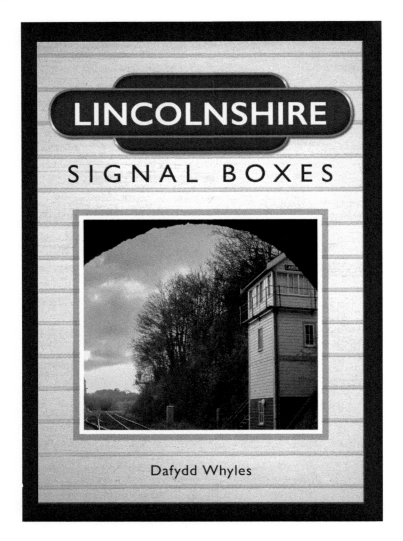

Lincolnshire Signal Boxes

Dafydd Whyles

Dafydd Whyles records the signal boxes of Lincolnshire before they
are closed for good.

978 1 4456 4812 5
96 pages, illustrated throughout

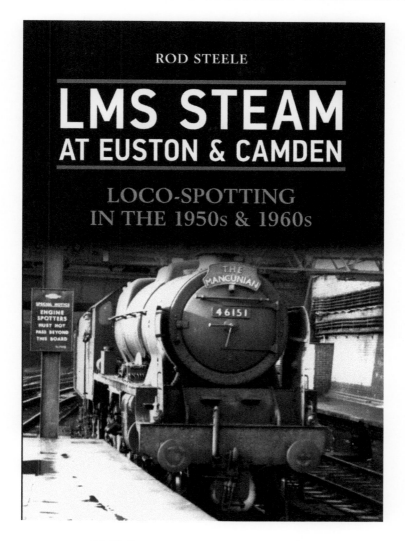

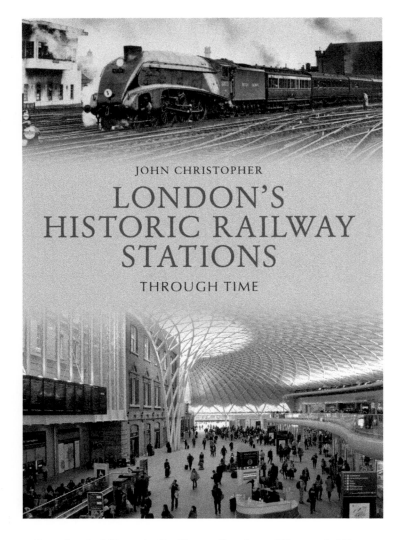

JOHN CHRISTOPHER

LONDON'S HISTORIC RAILWAY STATIONS

THROUGH TIME

London's Historic Railway Stations Through Time

John Christopher

This fascinating selection of photographs traces some of the many ways in which the capital's major railway stations have changed and developed over the years.

978 1 4456 5110 1

96 pages, illustrated throughout